Collins

Cambridge IGCSE™

Maths

WORKBOOK

Also for Cambridge IGCSE® (9–1)

Chris Pearce

William Collins' dream of knowledge for all began with the publication of his first book in 1819.
A self-educated mill worker, he not only enriched millions of lives, but also founded a flourishing publishing house.
Today, staying true to this spirit, Collins books are packed with inspiration, innovation and practical expertise.
They place you at the centre of a world of possibility and give you exactly what you need to explore it.

Collins. Freedom to teach.

Published by Collins
An imprint of HarperCollins*Publishers*
The News Building, 1 London Bridge Street, London, SE1 9GF, UK

HarperCollins*Publishers*
Macken House, 39/40 Mayor Street Upper, Dublin 1, D01 C9W8, Ireland

Browse the complete Collins catalogue at
collins.co.uk

© HarperCollins*Publishers* Limited 2024

10 9 8 7 6 5 4 3 2 1

ISBN 978-0-00-867084-9

Acknowledgements
With thanks to the following teachers for reviewing materials and providing valuable feedback: **Andrew Milne**, Ryedale School; **Sujatha Raghavan**, Manthan International School; and with thanks to the following teachers who provided feedback during the development stages: **Deepshikha Gupta**, Global City International School; **Mahesh Punjabi**; SVKM JV Parekh International School; **Pravin Yadav**, SVKM JV Parekh International School.

British Library Cataloguing-in-Publication Data
A catalogue record for this publication is available from the British Library.

Author: **Chris Pearce**
Expert reviewer: **Andrew Milne**
Publisher: **Elaine Higgleton**
Product manager: **Jennifer Hall**
Copyeditor: **Jim Newall**
Proofreader: **Laura Connell**
Cover designer: **Gordon MacGilp**
Cover artwork: **Ann Paganuzzi**
Internal designer and illustrator: **PDQ Media**
Typesetter: **PDQ Media**
Production controllers: **Sarah Hovell and Lyndsey Rogers**
Printed in India by Multivista Global Pvt. Ltd.

This book is produced from independently certified FSC™ paper to ensure responsible forest management. For more information visit:
www.harpercollins.co.uk/green

Cambridge International Education material in this publication is reproduced under licence and remains the intellectual property of Cambridge University Press & Assessment.

This text has not been through the endorsement process for the Cambridge Pathway. Any references or materials related to answers, grades, papers or examinations are based on the opinion of the author(s). The Cambridge International Education syllabus or curriculum framework associated assessment guidance material and specimen papers should always be referred to for definitive guidance.

The publishers gratefully acknowledge the permission granted to reproduce the copyright material in this book. Every effort has been made to trace copyright holders and to obtain their permission for the use of copyright material. The publishers will gladly receive any information enabling them to rectify any error or omission at the first opportunity.

Contents

E = **Extended**

Contents

Answers for all the questions in this Workbook are available from
http://www.collins.co.uk/internationalresources.

Multiples and factors

Student's Book pages 8–15 | Syllabus learning objectives C1.1; E1.1

....

1 23 24 25 26 27 28 29

From this list write down:

a a square number .... [1] **c** a multiple of 7 .... [1]

b a cube number .... [1] **d** a factor of 100 .... [1]

2 Find two square numbers with a sum of 45

.... [2]

3 Find the first five multiples of 13

.... [2]

4 Find the largest multiple of 6 that is less than 100

.... [2]

5 Find all the factors of 24

.... [2]

6 40 square tiles are arranged in a rectangle.

Describe two different ways to do this.

....

.... [2]

7 Find a factor of 56 that is not a multiple of 2

[2]

8 **a** Find the factors of 27

[1]

b Find the highest common factor of 27 and 45

[1]

9 **a** Write down the first 6 multiples of 8

[1]

b Find the lowest common multiple of 8 and 20

[1]

10 Here are four number cards.

| 1 | 2 | 6 | 8 |

a Put 2 cards together to make a square number.

[1]

b Put 3 cards together to make a cube number.

[1]

Prime numbers

Student's Book pages 15–21 | Syllabus learning objectives C1.1; E1.1

1   21   31   41   51   61

State the prime numbers in this list. ....   [2]

2   Show that 91 is not a prime number.

....   [1]

3   Find the value of $3^3 \times 2 + 3^2 \times 2^3$

....

....   [2]

4 $700 = 2^2 \times 5^2 \times 7$

Use this fact to write 2100 as a product of prime numbers.

....   [1]

5   Find the HCF of 48 and 80

....

....   [2]

6 $X = 2^3 \times 3^3 \times 7$ and $Y = 3^2 \times 7^2 \times 11$

Find the HCF of X and Y.

....   [2]

---

7 Work out the LCM of 36 and 54

[2]

8 Write 660 as a product of prime factors.

[3]

Rational and irrational numbers

Student's Book pages 20–21 | Syllabus learning objectives C1.1; E1.1

1 Find the reciprocal of:

TIP
The reciprocal of N is $\frac{1}{N}$

NO CALCULATOR

a 3 .... [1] **b** $3\frac{1}{2}$ .... [2]

2 Add the reciprocal of 2 and the reciprocal of 4

NO CALCULATOR

[2]

3 $\sqrt{4}$ $\sqrt{16}$ $\sqrt{24}$ $\sqrt{49}$ $\sqrt{100}$

NO CALCULATOR From the list write down:

a an irrational number .... [1] **b** an odd number .... [1]

c a square number .... [1]

4 Circle the irrational numbers in this list: $\sqrt{9}$ $\sqrt{19}$ $\sqrt{29}$ $\sqrt{39}$ $\sqrt{49}$ [1]

Fractions and decimals

Student's Book pages 24–27 | Syllabus learning objectives C1.4; E1.4

....

1 ▶ Simplify $\frac{54}{90}$ as much as possible.

.... [1]

2 ▶ Write $\frac{100}{12}$ as a mixed number as simply as possible.

.... [2]

3 ▶ Put these fractions in order of size, smallest first.

$\frac{3}{4}$ $\frac{2}{3}$ $\frac{5}{8}$ $\frac{1}{2}$

....

.... [2]

4 ▶ Write these decimals as fractions. Give your answers as simply as possible.

a 0.28 ....   **b** 0.375 .... [3]

5 ▶ Write these fractions as decimals.

a $\frac{5}{3}$ ....   **b** $\frac{3}{11}$ .... [3]

6 ▶ Put these numbers in order of size, smallest first.

$\frac{1}{3}$ 0.3 $\frac{2}{5}$ 0.28 $\frac{2}{9}$

....

.... [2]

Recurring decimals

Student's Book pages 28–30 | Syllabus learning objectives E1.4

1 ▶ Write $\frac{5}{6}$ as a recurring decimal.

[1]

2 ▶ Write $\frac{23}{9}$ as a recurring decimal.

[1]

3 ▶ Write each decimal as a mixed number.

a $4.\dot{6}$

[1]

b $6.\dot{4}$

[1]

4 ▶ Write $0.\dot{7}\dot{2}$ as a fraction as simply as possible.

[3]

5 ▶ a Write $0.3\dot{6}$ as a fraction as simply as possible.

[3]

b Write $0.1\dot{2}$ as a fraction.

[1]

Percentages, fractions and decimals

Student's Book pages 30–36 | Syllabus learning objectives C1.4; E1.4; C1.13; E1.13

1 Write each percentage as a fraction in its simplest form.

CALCULATOR

a 40% .... **b** 225% .... [3]

2 Write each percentage as a decimal.

CALCULATOR

a 7.5% .... **b** 180% .... [3]

3 **a** Sara scored 76 out of 80 in a mathematics test. Find her percentage mark.

CALCULATOR

.... [1]

b Malik scored 70% in the same test. How many marks did he get?

.... [1]

4 Work out:

CALCULATOR

a 10% of $25.70 .... [1]

b 75% of 60 kg .... [1]

c 150% of 3000 .... [1]

5 One month 1600 flights arrived at an airport.

18% were late arriving.

How many were **not** late?

.... [2]

6 Asher takes $250 out of a cash machine.

The cost of doing this is 1.6%.

Work out the cost in dollars.

.... [2]

7 Calculate these percentages of $764.00

a 83% of $764.00

.... [1]

b 6.7% of $764.00

.... [1]

c 139% of $764.00

.... [1]

Working with percentages

Student's Book pages 36–42 | Syllabus learning objectives C1.13; E 1.13

....

1 The price of a bike is $350.

a Find the new price after a 10% increase.

.... **[2]**

2 Kieran's salary is $32 400 per year. He is given a 4.5% increase.

Work out his new salary.

.... **[2]**

3 A tax of 22% is added to the price of new items.

The price of a phone before adding the tax is $380.

a Work out the price including the tax.

.... **[2]**

b If the tax is reduced to 17%, how much cheaper will the phone be?

.... **[2]**

4 A man has a mass of 114 kg. He reduces his mass by 8%.

Calculate his new mass. Give your answer to the nearest kg.

....

.... **[2]**

5 In an election, 5324 people were eligible to vote. Only 3018 actually voted.

Calculate the percentage that voted.

.... [1]

6 Maria bought a painting for $4600. Five years later she sold it for $10 300.

Calculate her percentage profit.

....

.... [2]

7 An electricity bill in January is $732

The bill in April is 10% higher than in January.

The bill in July is 5% higher than April.

Calculate the bill in July.

....

.... [3]

● ●

Interest

Student's Book pages 43–46 | Syllabus learning objectives C1.13; E1.13

● ●

1 A woman borrows $4000.

She pays 1.5% simple interest each month for 6 months.

How much interest does she pay in total?

.... [2]

2 Lara borrows $800. She pays 3% a year simple interest.

After n years she has paid $72 interest.

Find the value of n.

....

.... [2]

3 Sam puts $4000 in a savings account.

How much is it worth after 2 years if it earns:

a 6% per year simple interest

....

.... [2]

b 6% per year compound interest?

....

.... [2]

4 $2000 is put in a savings account.

It earns 7% per year compound interest.

a Fill in the missing numbers in this table. [2]

Time	Initially	After 1 year	After 2 years	After 3 years
Value	$2000		$2289.80	

b How much interest is earned in the third year?

.... [1]

5   Chen puts $25 000 in a savings account. He earns 8% per year compound interest.

How much is it worth after 6 years?

[2]

6   A man puts $5000 in a savings account. It earns 15% per year compound interest.

How many years will it take to double in value?

[2]

7   Carlos invests $18 000 and earns annual compound interest.

After 2 years the investment is worth $20 416.05. Calculate the annual rate of interest.

[2]

EXTENDED

Reverse percentages

Student's Book pages 47–49 | Syllabus learning objectives E1.13

1   The price of a cake is reduced by 25% to $12.60. Work out the original price.

[2]

2 The rent of an apartment increased by 5% to $2352 per month.

Work out the rent before the increase.

.... [2]

3 This week 384 people stayed in a hotel.

That is 40% fewer than last week. How many people stayed in the hotel last week?

....

.... [2]

4 The value of a house is $770 000. That is 120% more that its value 10 years ago.

Calculate the value 10 years ago.

....

.... [2]

5 The cost of a flight was increased by 5% and then by another 6%.

After these two increases the cost was $534.24

Calculate the cost before the increases.

....

.... [3]

Arithmetic operations

Student's Book pages 52–55 | Syllabus learning objectives C1.6; E1.6

1 Work out:

NO CALCULATOR

a $3 + 6 \times 4 =$ .... **b** $20 - 10 \div 5 =$ .... [2]

2 Work out:

NO CALCULATOR

a $2 \times 3 + 4 \times 5 =$ .... **b** $2 \times (3 + 4) \times 5 =$ .... [2]

3 Insert a pair of brackets to make this calculation correct.

NO CALCULATOR

$$20 - 16 - 11 - 7 = 8$$

.... [1]

4 In a kindergarten there must be at least one teacher for every 8 children.

NO CALCULATOR

a If there are 15 teachers, what is the maximum number of children the kindergarten can take?

.... [1]

b How many teachers are needed to look after 23 boys and 27 girls?

.... [2]

5 Tickets for a show cost $17 for adults and $11 for children.

Find the total cost for 8 adults and 12 children.

....

.... [2]

Fractions

Student's Book pages 55–63 | Syllabus learning objectives C1.6; E1.6

1 ▶ Work out:

a $\frac{3}{5}$ of 40 .... [1]

b $\frac{5}{7}$ of 42 .... [1]

2 ▶ Work out:

a $\frac{1}{4} + \frac{5}{8}$

.... [2]

b $\frac{1}{3} + \frac{2}{9}$

.... [2]

3 ▶ Work out:

a $\frac{1}{2} - \frac{1}{6}$

.... [2]

b $\frac{13}{16} - \frac{1}{4}$

.... [2]

4 ▶ Work out $2\frac{1}{2} + 1\frac{3}{4}$

.... [3]

5 ▶ Work out $\frac{1}{4} + \frac{2}{5}$

.... [2]

6 Work out $4\frac{3}{4} - 2\frac{1}{3}$

[4]

7 Work out the following. Write your answers as simply as possible.

a $\frac{2}{3} \times \frac{3}{4}$

[2]

b $\frac{2}{3} \div \frac{3}{4}$

[2]

8 Work out $\left(2\frac{1}{3}\right)^2$

[2]

9 Work out $3\frac{1}{4} \div 1\frac{1}{2}$

[2]

Negative numbers

Student's Book pages 66–75 | Syllabus learning objectives C1.6; E1.6

....

1 The temperature inside a house is 16.5 °C. The temperature outside is −4.0 °C.

Find the difference between these temperatures.

.... [1]

2 Mercury has a melting point of −39 °C. The boiling point is 357 °C.

Work out the difference between these two temperatures.

.... [1]

3 The temperature at 17:00 is 7 °C. The temperature falls by 4 °C every hour after that.

Work out the temperature at 20:00.

.... [1]

4 Here is a number line.

Write down the numbers A and B.

A is .... B is .... [2]

5 Work out:

a $4 + -5 =$ ....

b $-7 + 5 =$ .... [2]

6 Work out:

a $8 - -3 =$ ....

b $-4 - 5 =$ .... [2]

7 Work out $(7 - -6) - (9 + -5)$

.... [2]

8 Here is a subtraction: $13 - \ldots. = 20$

Work out the missing number.

.... [1]

9 The sum of two integers is 4. The difference between the integers is 8.

Work out the two integers.

....

.... [2]

10 Work out:

a $8 \div -4 = $ ....   **b** $-4 \div -8 = $ .... [2]

11 Work out $(12 \times -2) \div (-4 \times -3)$

....

.... [2]

Powers and roots

Student's Book pages 78–82 | Syllabus learning objectives C1.13; E1.13

1 Find the value of:

a $19^2 =$ ....

b $4.2^2 =$ ....

c $(-7)^2 =$ .... [3]

2 Write down:

a $\sqrt{225} =$ ....

b $\sqrt{15.21} =$ .... [2]

3 $x^2 = 50.41$

Write down the two possible values of x.

.... [2]

4 Work out $\sqrt{36 + 64}$

.... [1]

5 Write down:

a $8^3 =$ ....

b $2.1^3 =$ .... [2]

6 Calculate:

a $\sqrt[3]{729} =$ ....

b $\sqrt[3]{9.261} =$ .... [2]

7 Find the value of:

a $2^8 =$ ....

b $3^6 =$ ....

c $4^4 =$ .... [3]

8 ▶ Calculate:

a $\sqrt[4]{1296}$ = ...

b $\sqrt[5]{3125}$ = ...

c $\sqrt[6]{4096}$ = ...   [3]

9 ▶ 8^n = 32 768

Find the value of n.

....   [1]

10 ▶ n^3 = 729

> **TIP**
>
> First find the value of n.

Calculate the value of n^5.

....   [2]

11 ▶ Calculate $3 + 3^2 + 3^3 + 3^4$

....   [2]

Exponential growth
Student's Book pages 82–85 | Syllabus learning objectives E1.17

1 ▶ The cost of a holiday this year is $4000. The price increases by 5% each year. Calculate the price in three years.

....   [2]

2 ▶ The price of a new car is $26 000. The value decreases by 12% each year. Calculate the value in 4 years.

....   [2]

3 There is $2000 in a bank account. It earns 7% compound interest each year.

Calculate the number of years until it is worth $2800.

....

.... [2]

4 The population of a town is 32 000. The population is increasing by 1.2% per year.

Calculate the population in 10 years.

....

.... [2]

5 This table shows the number of visitors to a museum.

Year	2023	2024
Value	25 000	32 500

If the number of visitors is increasing exponentially, calculate the number of visitors in 2025.

....

.... [4]

Inequalities and Venn diagrams

Student's Book pages 88–93 | Syllabus learning objectives C1.5; E1.5; C1.2; E1.2

1 Here are three symbols: =, <, >

Write the correct symbol between each pair of values.

a $3 + 9$ .... $16 - 5$ **b** $40\,cm$ .... $4\,m$ **c** 6×4 .... 5^2 [3]

2 N is an integer and $-3 \leq N < 2$

Write down all the possible values of N.

.... [1]

3 Here is a Venn diagram.

List the elements of:

a X .... [1]

b $X \cup Y$ .... [1]

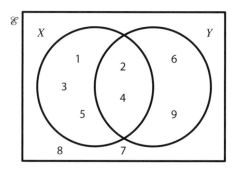

4 $\xi = \{\text{integer } x : 1 \leq x \leq 10\}, A = \{3, 5, 7\}, B = \{2, 5, 7, 10\}$

a   Put the elements in the Venn diagram.   [2]

b   Find $n(A \cap B)$. .... [1]

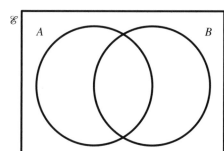

5 Write down:

a $n(R) =$ .... [1]

b $n(R \cup Q) =$ .... [1]

c $n(\xi) =$ .... [1]

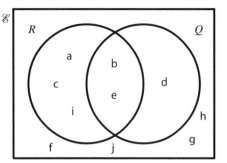

6 List the elements of:

a A' .... [1]

b $(A \cup B)'$ .... [1]

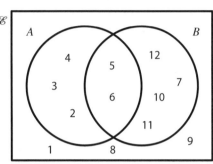

7 $\xi = \{$integer $x : 12 \leq x \leq 20\}$, $E = \{$even numbers$\}$, $T = \{$multiples of 3$\}$

a Put the numbers in the Venn diagram. [2]

b Find $n(E \cap T)$ .... [1]

c Find $n(E')$ .... [1]

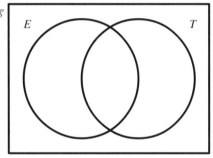

More Venn diagrams

Student's Book pages 93–99 | Syllabus learning objectives E1.2

1 This Venn diagram shows $\{$integer $x : 1 \le x \le 20\}$

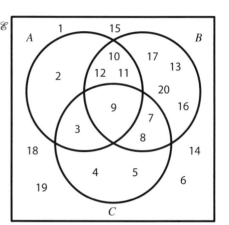

a List the elements of C.. [1]

b Find $n(A \cap B)$ .... [1]

c Find $n(A')$.. [1]

d List the elements of $A \cap B \cap C$........................... [1]

e Find $n(A \cup B \cup C)$....................................... [1]

f Shade on the diagram $A \cap (B \cup C)'$ [1]

2 $\xi = \{$integer $x : 1 \le x \le 30\}$

$E = \{$even numbers$\}$, $T = \{$multiples of 3$\}$, $F = \{$multiples of 5$\}$

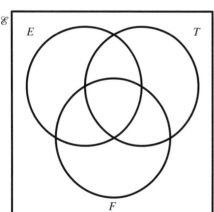

a Put the following numbers in the correct places on the Venn diagram.

26, 27, 28, 29, 30 [2]

b Write down a number in $E' \cap F$.. [1]

c Find $n(T \cap E)$.. [1]

3 $A = \{$multiples of 5$\}$, $B = \{$multiples of 7$\}$, $C = \{$multiples of 10$\}$

a Write down a possible value of x if $x \in A \cap B$

.... [1]

b Explain why $C \subset A$

....

.... [1]

c $P = \{$prime numbers$\}$

Explain why $C \cap P = \emptyset$ but $A \cap P \neq \emptyset$

....

.... [2]

Ratio

Student's Book pages 102–108 | Syllabus learning objectives C1.11; E1.11

....

1 Simplify each ratio as much as possible.

a 18 : 90 = ... [1]

b 16 : 12 : 8 = ... [1]

2 Ajay and Mona share some oranges in the ratio 2 : 3

a Find the fraction of the oranges that Ajay has.

.... [1]

b Mona has 12 more oranges than Ajay. How many oranges does Ajay have?

.... [2]

3 To make a drink you mix syrup and water in the ratio 1 : 5

a Find the amount of water you need to mix with 25 ml of syrup.

.... [1]

b Find the amount of syrup you need to make 480 ml of drink.

.... [1]

4 The ratio of men to women in a hall is 3 : 4

There are 36 men. Find the total number of people.

....

.... [2]

Rates and proportion

Student's Book pages 108–116 | Syllabus learning objectives C1.11; E1.11; C1.12; E1.12

....

1 A plane flies 2255 km in 2 hours 45 minutes. Calculate the average speed.

[2]

2 A car travels at an average speed of 72 km/h.

a Find the distance travelled in 3 hours 30 minutes.

[2]

b Find the time taken to travel 90 km. Give your answer in hours and minutes.

[2]

3 Fuel is flowing into the fuel tank of a car. The rate of flow is 0.8 litres per second.

Calculate the time to put 36 litres into the tank.

[1]

4 The mass of 340 cm^3 of aluminium is 918 g.

a Calculate the density of aluminium.

[1]

b Calculate the mass of $100 \, cm^3$ of aluminium.

.... [1]

5 The population of Indonesia is 268 million. The area of Indonesia is $1\,914\,000 \, km^2$.

Calculate the population density of Indonesia in people/km^2.

Round your answer to the nearest whole number.

....

.... [2]

6 A recipe for 30 cookies uses 225 g of flour.

a Work out how much flour you need to make 12 cookies.

....

.... [2]

b Calculate how many cookies you can make with 1 kg of flour.

....

.... [2]

7 60 text books cost $954

Calculate the cost of 175 textbooks.

....

.... [2]

Rounding numbers

Student's Book pages 120–124 | Syllabus learning objectives
C1.9; E1.9

1 **a** Round 626 to the nearest ten. .... [1]

b Round 78 709 to the nearest hundred. .... [1]

2 The population of a town is 23 266

Round this number to the nearest thousand. .... [1]

3 $3\frac{1}{7} = 3.142857\ldots$

a Round this number to 1 decimal place. .... [1]

b Round this number to 3 decimal places. .... [1]

4 Round these numbers to 1 significant figure.

a 62 845= .... **b** 4.9023 = ... [1]

5 Round these numbers to 3 significant figures.

a 2.828 282 = ... **b** 104 891 = ... [1]

6 $\frac{1}{483} = 0.002070393\ldots$

Round this number to 3 significant figures. .... [1]

Estimating answers

Student's Book pages 124–128 | Syllabus learning objectives C1.9; E1.9; C1.10; E1.10

1 ▷ Here is a multiplication: 38.25×21.75

Round each number to the nearest ten to find an estimate of the answer.

.... [2]

2 ▷ The population of a town is 54 000 to the nearest thousand.

Write down the largest possible population of the town.

.... [1]

3 ▷ The length of a line, to the nearest millimetre, is 13.0 cm.

Write down the upper bound .... [1]

4 ▷ An athlete runs a race in 21.35 s.

The time is rounded to 2 decimal places.

Write down the upper and lower bounds of the time.

.... [2]

5 ▷ The mass of a car is 1600 kg, to 2 significant figures.

Find the upper and lower limits of the mass.

.... [2]

6 $\dfrac{63.8}{6.073 \times 4.831}$

Estimate the answer to this calculation.

....

.... **[2]**

7 A cyclist travels for 7 hours 53 minutes at an average speed of 28.9 km/h.

Estimate the distance travelled.

.... **[2]**

8 The side of a square is measured as 21.1 m.

a Find an upper bound for the length of each side. .... **[1]**

b Find an upper bound for the perimeter of the square. .... **[1]**

● ●

EXTENDED # Bounds for calculations

Student's Book pages 128–131 | Syllabus learning objectives E1.10

....

1 The mass of a book is 280 g to the nearest 10 g.

Calculate the upper bound for the total mass of 24 books.

.... **[2]**

2 The average speed of a train is 113 km/h to the nearest whole number.

Find a lower bound for the distance travelled in one minute. Give your answer in metres.

....

.... [3]

3 The sides of a rectangle are 7.5 cm and 18 cm to 2 significant figures..

Calculate upper and lower bounds for the area of the rectangle.

....

.... [4]

TIP
density $= \dfrac{\text{mass}}{\text{volume}}$

4 The mass of a piece of aluminium is 12.2 g and the volume is 4.5 cm^3.

Both values are correct to 1 decimal place.

Calculate an upper bound for the density of aluminium.

.... [2]

5 A tank holds 2500 litres of water.

Water is flowing out at a rate of 17 litres per second.

Both these numbers are correct to 2 significant figures.

Calculate the shortest time it will take to empty the tank.

.... [2]

Standard form

Student's Book pages 134–139 | Syllabus learning objectives C1.8; E1.8

1 Write these numbers in standard form.

a 315 000 = ... [1] **b** 90 million = ... [1]

2 Write these numbers in standard form.

a 0.002 05 = ... [1] **b** 43×10^{-6} = ... [1]

3 Write these numbers in full.

a 5.72×10^4 = ... [1] **b** 3.1×10^{-5} = ... [1]

4 The average distance from the Earth to the Sun is 151 400 000 km.

Write this distance in standard form. .... [1]

5 The diameter of a human blood cell is about 0.000 007 5 m.

Write this number in standard form. .... [1]

Standard form without a calculator

Student's Book pages 140–142 | Syllabus learning objectives E1.8

1 $A = 8.5 \times 10^7$ and $B = 3.9 \times 10^6$

a Work out $A + B$ and give your answer in standard form.

[2]

b Work out $A - B$ and give your answer in standard form.

[2]

2 Multiply 3.1×10^5 by 6×10^4. Give your answer in standard form.

[2]

3 Work out:

a $(8 \times 10^{20}) \div (2 \times 10^5)$ .... [1]

b $(8 \times 10^{20}) \div (2 \times 10^{-5})$ .... [1]

4 The population of Brazil is 2×10^8 people.

The area of Brazil is $8 \times 10^6 \, \text{km}^2$.

Work out the population density of Brazil.

....

.... [2]

5 $X = 1.2 \times 10^{-3}$ and $Y = 4 \times 10^9$

Work out the following. Give your answers in standard form.

a $X \times Y$

.... [2]

b $X \div Y$

.... [2]

6 The area of India is $3.29 \times 10^6 \, \text{km}^2$.

The area of Pakistan is $8.0 \times 10^5 \, \text{km}^2$.

a Work out the total area of the two countries. Write your answer in standard form.

.... [2]

b Find a whole number to complete this sentence:

The area of India is approximately .... times the area of Pakistan.

.... [2]

Surds

Student's Book pages 142–147 | Syllabus learning objectives E1.18

1 Simplify

a $\sqrt{2} \times \sqrt{18}$ .... [2]

b $\sqrt{5} \times \sqrt{20}$ .... [2]

2 Write $\sqrt{50}$ in the form $a\sqrt{2}$ where a is an integer.

.... [2]

3 Simplify as much as possible $\sqrt{2} \times \sqrt{3} \times \sqrt{5}$

.... [2]

4 Simplify $\sqrt{2}(\sqrt{2} + \sqrt{72})$

....

.... [2]

5 Multiply the brackets and simplify

a $(4 + \sqrt{3})^2$

....

.... [3]

b $(3 + \sqrt{7})(3 - \sqrt{7})$

....

.... [2]

6 Show that $\sqrt{20} + \sqrt{45} = 5\sqrt{5}$

....

.... [2]

7 Rationalise the denominator of $\dfrac{10}{\sqrt{2}}$

....

.... [2]

8 Simplify $\dfrac{\sqrt{3}}{\sqrt{48}}$

....

.... [2]

HINT
Rationalise the denominator of your answer

9 Find the reciprocal of $3 + \sqrt{5}$

....

.... [2]

10 Rationalise the denominator of $\dfrac{1 + \sqrt{3}}{2 + \sqrt{3}}$. Simplify the answer as much as possible.

....

.... [3]

Units

Student's Book pages 150–158 | Syllabus learning objectives C5.1, E5.1; C1.15; E1.15; C1.16; E1.16; C1.14; E1.14

....

1 A bottle contains 0.7 litres of a drink. Write this in millilitres.

NO CALCULATOR

0.7 litres = ... ml [1]

2 Work out the total of 6.5 m and 180 cm.

NO CALCULATOR

.... [1]

3 The mass of a car is 1.84 tonnes. Change this to kilograms.

NO CALCULATOR

.... [1]

4 A diver holds his breath for 13 minutes. Write this time in seconds.

.... [1]

5 Here is the timetable for two trains.

	Depart	Arrive
First train	09 45	10 32
Second train	10 20	13 15

a Work out the journey time for the first train.

.... [1]

b Work out the journey time for the second train.

.... [1]

6 A plane leaves Madrid at 19 30. It is going to Dubai. The flight takes 7 hours 10 minutes.

Dubai is 3 hours ahead of Madrid.

Work out the time in Dubai when the plane arrives.

....

.... [2]

7 An exchange rate is 1 US dollar = 4.98 Brazilian reals.

a Change 56.25 US dollars into reals.

.... [2]

b Change 850 reals into US dollars.

.... [2]

8

a Calculate $\dfrac{700}{3.14 \times 45}$ and write down all the digits in your answer.

.... [1]

b Round your answer to 2 significant figures. .... [1]

9 Calculate $\sqrt{41.4^2 + 55.2^2}$

.... [2]

10 Show that 1 million seconds is about $11\dfrac{1}{2}$ days.

....

.... [2]

Formulas

Student's Book pages 172–179 | Syllabus learning objectives C2.1; E2.1; C2.5

1 Greta is n years old. Ivan is 3 years older than Greta. Jan is twice as old as Ivan.

a Write an expression for Ivan's age. .... [1]

b Write an expression for Jan's age. .... [1]

2 Ants have 6 legs and spiders have 8 legs.

Write an expression for the total number of legs on x ants and y spiders.

.... [1]

3 The length of a rectangle is l cm and the width is w cm.

a Write an expression for the perimeter of the rectangle in centimetres.

.... [1]

b Write an expression for the perimeter of the rectangle in **millimetres**.

.... [1]

4 Chen buys concert tickets.

Each ticket costs $20. There is a booking fee of $4

a Find the total cost when Chen buys 6 tickets. .... [1]

b Write a formula for the cost (C) of n tickets. .... [1]

5 Here is a formula: $y = 5x - 3$

a Find the value of y when $x = 4$

.... [1]

b Find the value of y when $x = -4$

.... [1]

c Rearrange the formula to make x the subject.

.... [2]

6 $x = 10$

a Find the value of $x^2 - 6$

.... [2]

b Find the value of $(x - 6)^2$

.... [2]

7 $v = 20t + 12$

Rearrange the formula to make t the subject.

.... [2]

8 $m = \dfrac{a + b}{2}$

Rearrange the formula to make a the subject.

.... [2]

EXTENDED

More formulas

Student's Book pages 179–181 | Syllabus learning objectives E2.5

1 $y = x^2 + 3$

Make x the subject of this formula.

[2]

2 Here is a formula: $s = \frac{1}{2}at^2$

a Make a the subject of the formula.

[2]

b Make t the subject of the formula.

[2]

3 Here is a formula: $t = 2\sqrt{\dfrac{l}{g}}$

Rearrange the formula to make l the subject.

[2]

Simplifying expressions

Student's Book pages 184–194 | Syllabus learning objectives C2.2; E2.2

1 Simplify:

a $6c \times 4$ .... [1]

b $3d \times 5d$ .... [1]

2 Simplify as much as possible.

a $x + 2y + 3x - 5y$ .... [1]

b $7 + 2t - 6 + 8t$ .... [1]

3 Expand each expression.

a $3(2d - 7)$ .... [1]

b $4(3 + 5t)$ .... [1]

c $a(8a - 10)$ .... [1]

4 Expand each expression and simplify it as much as possible.

a $2(x - 3) + 3(x - 5)$

....

.... [3]

b $5(y + 2) - 4(y - 1)$

....

.... [3]

5 Factorise each expression as much as possible.

a $10x + 30$ .... [2]

b $16a - 12$ .... [2]

c $6ac + 9bc - 3c$ .... [2]

d $4a^2 + 8ab - 8ac$ .... [2]

6 Find the highest common factor of a^3bc and a^2b^2

.... [2]

Multiplying two brackets

Student's Book pages 195–200 | Syllabus learning objectives C2.2; E2.2

1 Expand and simplify $(x + 3)(x + 5)$

....

.... [3]

2 Expand and simplify $(x - 4)(x + 1)$

....

.... [3]

3 Expand and simplify $(t - 3)(t - 6)$

....

.... [3]

4 Expand and simplify $(8 + d)(3 - d)$

[3]

5 Expand and simplify $(3x + 2)(x + 4)$

[3]

6 Expand and simplify $(2x + 1)(3x + 1)$

[3]

7 Expand and simplify $(4x - 5)(5x + 4)$

[3]

8 Expand and simplify $(t + 4)^2$

[3]

9 Expand and simplify $(3x - 2)^2$

[3]

10 Expand and simplify $(y + 10)(y - 10)$

....

.... [3]

11 Expand and simplify $(x + 3)^2 + (x - 3)^2$

....

.... [4]

• •

Brackets and factorisation

Student's Book pages 200–209 | Syllabus learning objectives E2.2

1 **a** Expand and simplify $(x + 6)(x - 5)$

....

.... [2]

b Expand $x(x + 6)(x - 5)$

.... [1]

2 Expand and simplify $(x + 1)(x - 2)(x + 3)$

....

....

.... [4]

3 Factorise $x^2 + 8x + 12$

[2]

4 Factorise $y^2 - y - 20$

[2]

5 Factorise $2x^2 + 5x - 12$

[3]

6 Factorise $x^2 + 2xy - 15y^2$

[3]

7 Factorise $9x^2 - 4y^2$

[2]

8 **a** Factorise $x^3 + 2x^2 + x$

[3]

b Factorise $x^3 - 16x$

[3]

9 Write $x^2 + 8x + 20$ in completed square form.

[3]

10 Write $x^2 - 5x + 11$ in completed square form.

[3]

Algebraic fractions

Student's Book pages 209–212 | Syllabus learning objectives E2.3

1 Simplify $\frac{x}{2} + \frac{x-1}{3}$

[3]

2 Simplify as much as possible $\frac{2a^2}{5} \div \frac{a}{10}$

[3]

3 Write as a single fraction $\dfrac{1}{x-3} + \dfrac{1}{x+3}$

[3]

4 Simplify $\dfrac{x+1}{x} - \dfrac{x+2}{x+1}$

[4]

5 Simplify as much as possible $\dfrac{x^2+x-6}{x^2+2x-8}$

[4]

Linear equations

Student's Book pages pages 216–224 | Syllabus learning objectives C2.5; E2.5

1 Solve the equation $4x - 6 = 26$

[2]

2 Solve the equation $10(y + 3) = 75$

[2]

3 Solve the equation $\dfrac{2t - 5}{4} = 3$

[3]

4 Solve the equation $20 - 2x = 9$

[3]

5 Solve the equation $2x + 14 = 6$

[2]

6 Solve the equation $5x - 7 = 3x + 9$

[3]

7 Solve the equation $3x + 4 = 19 - 2x$

[3]

8 The perimeter of this shape is 55 cm.

x cm

$x + 2$ cm

$x + 3$ cm

$x + 4$ cm

a Write down an equation to show this.

.... [1]

b Find the length of the longest side of the shape.

.... [3]

9 Hassan is thinking of three consecutive odd numbers.

The smallest odd number is N.

a Write down expressions for the other two odd numbers.

.... [1]

The sum of the three odd numbers is 231.

b Work out the value of N.

....

.... [3]

10 Solve the equation $5(x - 3) = 3(x + 3)$

....

.... [3]

Quadratic equations

Student's Book pages 224–234 | Syllabus learning objectives E2.5

1 Solve the equation $x^2 + x - 12 = 0$

NO CALCULATOR

[2]

2 Solve the equation $x^2 - 10x + 21 = 0$

NO CALCULATOR

[4]

3 Solve the equation $3x^2 + 4x - 4 = 0$

NO CALCULATOR

[4]

4 **a** Solve the equation $x(2x + 1) = 0$

NO CALCULATOR

[2]

b Solve the equation $x(2x + 1) = 3$

[4]

5 **a** Solve the equation $9x^2 - 1 = 0$

NO CALCULATOR

[2]

b   Solve the equation $9x^2 + 1 = 6x$

[3]

6   Solve the equation $x^2 - 3x - 2 = 0$

TIP
The solution of the equation $ax^2 + bx + c = 0$ is $$x = \frac{-b \pm \sqrt{b^2 - 4ac}}{2a}$$

Round your answers to 2 decimal places.

[4]

7   **a**   Write $x^2 - 6x$ in completed square form.

LCULATOR

[2]

b   Find the **exact** solutions of the equation $x^2 - 6x = 2$

[3]

EXTENDED   NO CALCULATOR

Fractional equations

Student's Book pages 234–236 | Syllabus learning objectives E2.5

1   Solve the equation $\dfrac{9t + 10}{2t} = 6$

[3]

2 ▶ Solve the equation $\dfrac{5}{x-1} = \dfrac{9}{x+1}$

....

.... [3]

3 ▶ Solve the equation $\dfrac{2x}{x+1} + \dfrac{1}{x-1} = 2$

....

.... [5]

● ●

Simultaneous equations

Student's Book pages 236–244 | Syllabus learning objectives C2.5; E2.5

....

1 ▶ Solve these simultaneous equations: $x + y = 24$ $y = 3x$

....

.... [3]

2 ▶ Solve these simultaneous equations: $y = 2x - 5$ $y = x + 4$

....

.... [3]

3 ▶ The sum of two numbers is 20. The difference between them is 4.

Find the two numbers.

....

.... [3]

4 Solve these simultaneous equations: $x = y - 9$ $y = 2x + 5$

[3]

5 Solve these simultaneous equations: $x + y = 12$ $x + 2y = 20$

[3]

6 Solve these simultaneous equations: $2x + y = 22$ $2x - y = 14$

[3]

7 Solve these simultaneous equations: $y = 3x - 8$ $y = 10 - x$

[3]

8 Solve these simultaneous equations: $3x + y = 13$ $x + 2y = 1$

[4]

9 Solve these simultaneous equations: $2x + 3y = 26$ $3x - 2y = 13$

[4]

EXTENDED

Non-linear simultaneous equations

Student's Book pages 244–246 | Syllabus learning objectives E2.5

1 ▶ Solve this pair of equations: $x + y = 6$ $x^2 + y^2 = 18$

[5]

2 ▶ Solve this pair of simultaneous equations: $xy = 10$ $y = x + 3$

[5]

3 ▶ The equation of a circle is $x^2 + y^2 = 80$

The equation of a straight line is $y = 2x$

Find the coordinates of the points where the straight line intersects the circle.

[4]

4 Solve this pair of equations simultaneously: $y = 4x + 16$ $y = (x + 1)^2$

....

....

....

.... **[5]**

Representing inequalities

Student's Book pages 247–248 | Syllabus learning objectives C2.5; E2.5

1 $-4 \leq x < 3$

Show this inequality on the number line.

[2]

2 {integer n: $5 < n < 10$}

Write down all the elements of this set.

.... **[2]**

3 Myra is x years old. Chen is y years old.

Write inequalities to show that:

a Myra is more than 12 years old .... **[1]**

b Chen is older than Myra .... **[1]**

c the sum of their ages is less than 30 .... **[1]**

4 The point (x, y) is inside the square.

a Write an inequality for x

.... [1]

b Write an inequality for y

.... [1]

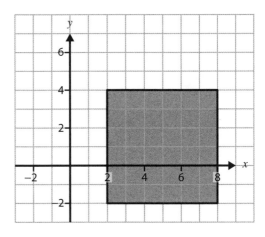

• •

EXTENDED # Solving inequalities

Student's Book pages 249–252 | Syllabus learning objectives E2.6

1 **a** Solve the inequality $4x - 7 \leq 15$

.... [2]

b Show your solution on the number line.

```
├─────────────────────────┬─────────────────────────┤
                          0
```
[2]

2 Solve the inequality $3x - 12 > x + 6$

....

.... [2]

3 Solve the inequality $3 \leq 2x + 9 \leq 33$

....

.... [3]

4 Solve the inequality $20 - x \geq 2x + 12$

....

.... **[3]**

5 The perimeter of this quadrilateral is at least 100 cm.

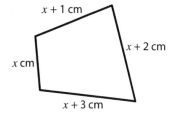

$x + 1$ cm

$x + 2$ cm

x cm

$x + 3$ cm

a Write an inequality for x

.... **[1]**

b Solve your inequality.

....

.... **[2]**

6 Solve the inequality $-3 \leq 2(5x - 1) < 3$

....

.... **[3]**

7 Solve the inequality $3(x + 5) \leq 7(5 - x)$

....

.... **[3]**

Practical graphs

Student's Book pages 256–259 | Syllabus learning objectives C2.9; E2.9

1

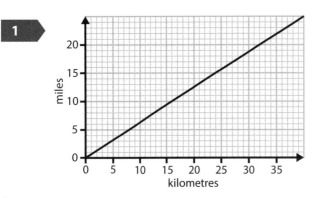

This a conversion graph between miles and kilometres. Use the graph to change:

a   25 km to miles .... [1]

b   10 miles to kilometres .... [1]

2

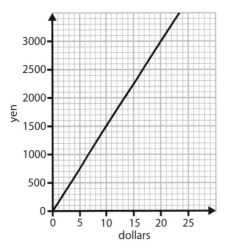

This is a conversion graph between dollars and yen. Use the graph to change:

a   16 dollars to yen .... [1]

b   1700 yen to dollars .... [1]

3 Maria goes for a walk. It takes 4.5 hours. The graph shows her journey.

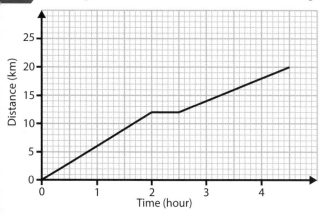

a How far did Maria walk? .... [1]

b Work out Maria's average speed for the first two hours.

.... [2]

c Maria stopped for a rest. How many minutes did she rest?

.... [1]

d Work out Maria's average speed for the last part of her journey.

.... [2]

4 A car starts a journey at 11:00. It travels for 2 hours at an average speed of 40 km/h.
Then it stops for 90 minutes. Then it travels at an average speed of 60 km/h until 17:00.

a Show the journey on a graph. [4]

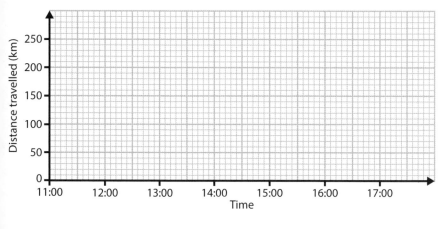

b Write down the distance the car travels .... [1]

Further practical graphs

Student's Book pages 264–271 | Syllabus learning objectives E2.9

1 A car accelerates from rest and then travels at a constant speed before slowing to a stop.

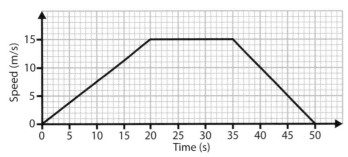

a Find the acceleration for the first 20 seconds.

.... [2]

b Find the deceleration for the last 15 seconds.

.... [2]

c Find the total distance travelled.

.... [2]

2

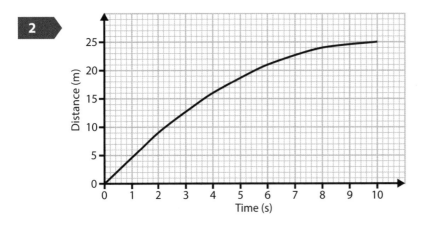

The graph shows the distance travelled by a person walking.

a   Find the distance travelled after 6 seconds. .... [1]

b   Estimate the speed after 6 seconds.

.... [3]

TIP
Draw a tangent to find the gradient

c   Explain how the graph shows that the walker is slowing down.

.... [3]

3

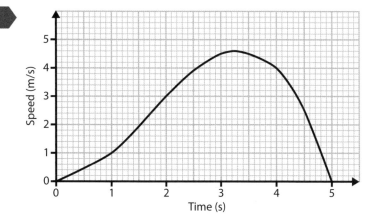

The graph shows the speed of a runner over a 5-second interval.

a   Estimate the acceleration after 2 seconds.

.... [3]

b   Estimate the deceleration after 4.5 seconds.

.... [3]

Straight-line graphs

Student's Book pages 274–281 | Syllabus learning objectives C3.1; E3.1; C3.2; E3.2; C3.3; E3.3; C3.5; E3.5

....

1 **a** Complete this table of values. [2]

x	−3	−2	−1	0	1	2	3	4
$0.5x + 1$		0				2		

b Draw a graph of $y = 0.5x + 1$ [2]

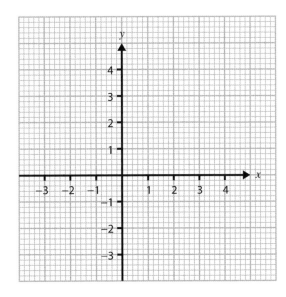

c Find the gradient of the line. .... [1]

2 The equation of a line is $y = 4x − 20$

a Where does the line cross the y-axis? .... [1]

b Find the gradient of the line. .... [1]

c Where does the line cross the x-axis?

.... [2]

3 The gradient of a straight line is 8

The line crosses the y-axis at (0, 5)

a Write down the equation of the line.

.... [1]

b The line passes through the point (6, n)

Find the value of n

.... [2]

4

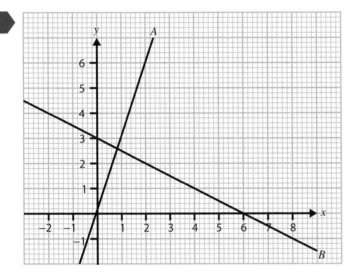

a Find the gradient of line A.

.... [2]

b Find the equation of line A.

.... [1]

c Find the equation of line B.

....

.... [3]

More straight-line graphs

Student's Book pages 281–283 | Syllabus learning objectives E3.2

1 The equation of a line is $2x + 3y = 12$

a Where does the line cross the y-axis?

[2]

b Where does the line cross the x-axis?

[2]

c Find the gradient of the line.

[1]

2 The equation of a line is $2y = 4 - x$

a Find the gradient of the line.

[2]

b Where does the line cross the y-axis?

[1]

3 The equation of a straight line is $8x + 4y + 11 = 0$

a Find the gradient of the line.

[2]

b Find the intercept on the y-axis.

.... [2]

c The line passes through the point $(-3, a)$

Find the value of a.

.... [3]

4 Find the equation of this line.

....

....

....

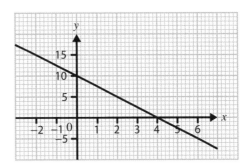

[3]

● ●

Solving equations graphically

Student's Book pages 283–290 | Syllabus learning objectives C2.10; E2.10; C3.6; E3.6

....

1 This is a graph of $y = 4x + 10$

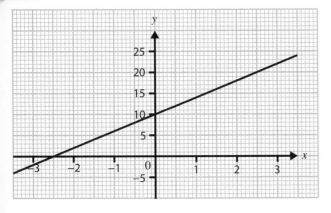

Use the graph to solve these equations.

a $4x + 10 = 16$

.... [1]

a $4x + 10 = 3$.

.... [1]

71

2 This graph shows the line $5x + 8y = 30$

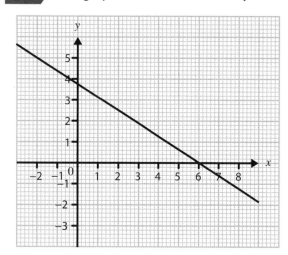

a On the same axes draw the line $y = 2x - 1$

....

.... [4]

b Use the graph to solve the equations $5x + 8y = 30$ and $y = 2x - 1$ simultaneously.

$x = $ .... and $y = $ .... [2]

3

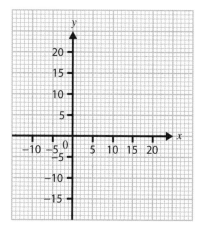

a Draw a graph of $y = 20 - x$

....

.... [3]

b Draw a parallel line through the point (–10, 15)

.... [2]

c Find the equation of the second line.

.... [2]

4 The equation of a straight line is $y = 15x$

a Find the equation of a parallel line that has the y-intercept (0, 30)

.... [2]

b Find the equation of a parallel line that passes through (3, 0)

.... [2]

Points and lines

EXTENDED

Student's Book pages 288–292 | Syllabus learning objectives E3.3; E3.4; E3.7

1

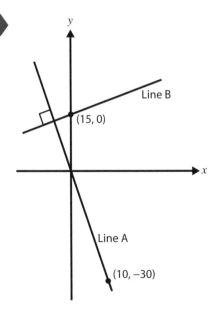

Line A and line B are perpendicular.

a Find the equation of line A.

[3]

b Find the equation of line B.

[3]

2 Find the equation of the straight line through (5, 0) and (0, −8)

[3]

3 A is (4, 1) and B is (10, 9)

a Find the midpoint of AB.

[2]

b Calculate the length of the line segment AB.

[3]

c Find the equation of the perpendicular bisector to AB.

[4]

4 P is (4, –4) and Q is (7, 8)

Find the equation of the straight line through P and Q.

....

....

....

....

.... [5]

5 A straight line is perpendicular to $2x + y = 20$

It passes through (4, 12)

Find the equation of the line.

....

....

....

....

.... [5]

Quadratic graphs

Student's Book pages 296–302 | Syllabus learning objectives C2.10; E2.10

1 **a** Complete this table. [2]

x	−4	−3	−2	−1	0	1	2	3	4
$10 - x^2$		1							−6

b Use the table to draw a graph of $y = 10 - x^2$ [3]

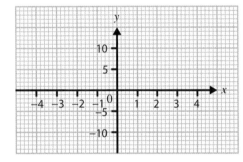

c Use the graph to solve the equation $10 - x^2 = 4$

[2]

d On the graph draw the straight line $y = 5x$ [2]

e Use the graph to find a positive solution of the equation $10 - x^2 = 5x$

[1]

2 **a** Complete this table. [2]

x	−3	−2	−1	0	1	2	3	4
$x^2 - x - 3$		3				−1		

b Draw a graph of $y = x^2 - x - 3$ [3]

c Use the graph to solve the equation $x^2 = x + 3$

.... [2]

3 **a** Complete this table. [2]

x	−3	−2	−1	0	1	2	3	4	5
x^2		4		0				16	
$3x + 4$		−2		4				16	

b Draw a graph of $y = x^2$ [3]

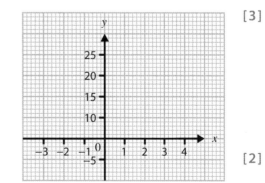

c On the same graph draw the straight line $y = 3x + 4$ [2]

d Solve the equation $x^2 = 3x + 4$

.... [2]

EXTENDED

Turning points

Student's Book pages 303–304 | Syllabus learning objectives E2.11

1 **a** Write $x^2 - 6x$ in complete square form.

.... [2]

b Find the turning point of the graph of $y = x^2 - 6x$

.... [2]

c Sketch a graph of $y = x^2 - 6x$

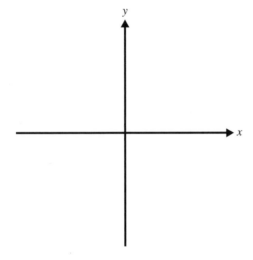

[3]

2 **a** Find the turning point on the graph of $y = 100 - x^2$

.... [2]

b Sketch the graph of $y = 100 - x^2$ [3]

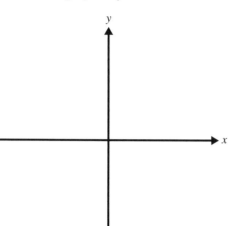

● ●

Reciprocal graphs

Student's Book pages 304–306 | Syllabus learning objectives C2.10

1 **a** Complete this table of values. [2]

x	−4	−3	−2	−1	−0.5	0.5	1	2	3	4
$\dfrac{2}{x}$				−2					0.67	

b Draw a graph of $y = \dfrac{2}{x}$ for $-4 \le x \le 4$ [3]

c On the same axes draw a graph of $y = x + 1$ [2]

d Use your graph to solve the equation $\dfrac{2}{x} = x + 1$

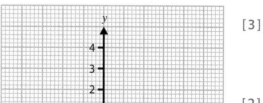

....

.... [2]

2 **a** Complete this table of values. [2]

x	0.5	1	2	3	4	5
$\dfrac{10}{x}$				3.33		

b Draw a graph of $y = \dfrac{10}{x}$ for $-5 \leq x \leq 5$. [3]

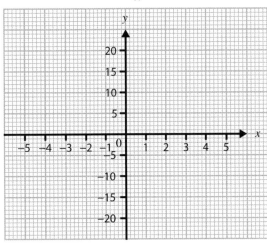

c On the same axes draw a graph of $y = 5x$ [2]

d Use your graph to solve the equation $\dfrac{10}{x} = 5x$

[2]

More graphs

Student's Book pages 306–316 | Syllabus learning objectives E2.10

1 **a** Complete this table. Round the values to 1 d.p. [2]

x	0	20	40	60	80	100
$4 + 2\sqrt{x}$			16.6			

b Draw a graph of $y = 4 + 2\sqrt{x}$ for $0 \leq x \leq 100$ [3]

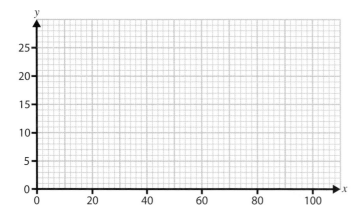

c By drawing a straight line on the graph solve the equation $x + 4\sqrt{x} = 32$

....

.... [4]

2 **a** Complete this table of values. [2]

x	0	1	2	3	4
3×2^x			12		

b   Draw a graph of $y = 3 \times 2^x$ for $0 \leq x \leq 4$ [3]

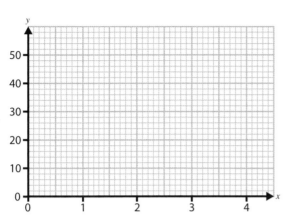

[3]

c   Solve the equation $3 \times 2^x = 20$

.... [2]

d   By drawing a suitable straight line, solve the equation $2^x + 4x = 12$

....

.... [4]

● ●

EXTENDED

Gradients of curves

Student's Book pages 316–318 | Syllabus learning objectives E2.12

· ·

1

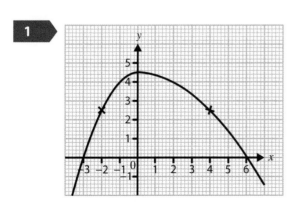

a   Draw a tangent to the curve at $(-2, 2.5)$ [2]

b   Estimate the gradient of the curve at (−2, 2.5)

.... [2]

c   Draw a tangent to the curve at (4, 2.5)   [2]

d   Find the equation of the tangent at (4, 2.5)

....

.... [3]

2 ▶ **a**   Complete this table of values.   [1]

x	0	1	4	9	16	25	36
$\sqrt{x}$					4		6

b   Draw a graph of $y = \sqrt{x}$ [1]

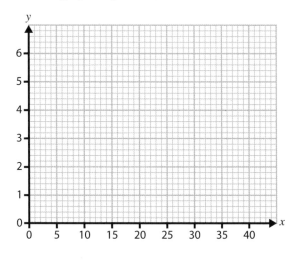

c   Estimate the gradient of the curve at (16, 4)

> **TIP**
>
> The scales on the axes are not identical

.... [3]

d   By drawing a suitable straight line, solve the equation $x + 5\sqrt{x} = 25$

....

.... [3]

Number sequences

Student's Book pages 322–334 | Syllabus learning objectives C2.7; E2.7

....

1 **a** Find the next two numbers in this sequence.

17, 21, 25, 29, ..., ... [2]

b What is the rule for the sequence:

.... [1]

2 Here is the start of a sequence: 8, 16, 24, 32, 40, …

Find the largest number in the sequence that is less than 100.

.... [2]

3 Here is the start of a sequence: 0, 3, 8, 15, 24, …

HINT
Think about square numbers.

a Find the next number in the sequence. .... [1]

b Find the 10th number in the sequence. .... [1]

4 The nth term in a sequence is $3n + 5$.

a Find the 4th term. .... [1]

b Find the 20th term. .... [1]

5 The nth term in a sequence is $2n^2 + 1$.

a Find the 1st term. .... [1]

b Find the 5th term. .... [1]

6 Find the *n*th term of each sequence.

a 1, 8, 27, 64, 125 .... [1]

b 5, 12, 31, 68, 129 .... [1]

7 Each line in these patterns is 1 cm long.

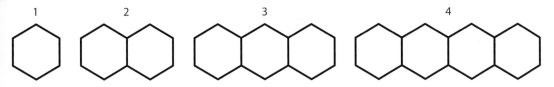

1   2   3   4

a Complete this table.

Pattern	1	2	3	4
Perimeter (cm)		10		

[1]

b Find the perimeter of the 5th pattern. .... [1]

c Find the perimeter of the *n*th pattern. .... [1]

EXTENDED

Further number sequences

Student's Book pages 334–337 | Syllabus learning objectives E2.7

1 Find the nth term of this sequence.

100, 97, 94, 91, 88, …

[2]

2 The nth term of a sequence is 2.5×4^n. Find:

a the first term .... [1]

b the fourth term. .... [1]

3 Find the nth term of each sequence.

a 0.5, 2, 4.5, 8, 12.5, …

[2]

b 1.5, 4, 7.5, 12, 17.5, …

[2]

4 These are the first four rectangles in a sequence.

The rectangles are divided into centimetre squares.

a Find the area of the 5th rectangle in cm^2.

.... [1]

b Find the area of the nth rectangle in cm^2.

....

.... [3]

5 The nth term of a sequence is $n^2 + an + b$ where a and b are integers.

a The first term is 11. Show that $a + b = 10$

....

.... [2]

b The second term is 18. Work out the values of a and b.

....

....

.... [4]

Indices

NO CALCULATOR

Student's Book pages 340–346 | Syllabus learning objectives
C1.17; E1.17; C2.4; E2.4

1 **a** Write 64 as a power of 4. .... [1]

b Write 64 as a power of 2. .... [1]

2 $3^5 = 243$. Use this fact to find 3^6

.... [2]

3 Find:

a $20^0 =$ .... [1]

b $20^3 =$ .... [1]

4 Write as a fraction:

a $4^{-2} =$ .... [1]

b $2^{-5} =$ .... [1]

c $5^{-3} =$ .... [1]

5 Write as a power of 6.

a $6^5 \times 6^4$ .... [1]

b $6^{12} \div 6^3$ .... [1]

6 Write as a power of 2.

a 4^5

.... [2]

b $8^6 \times 2^3$

.... [2]

c $\dfrac{2^5 \times 4^2}{8^2}$

.... [2]

7 Write as a power of a.

a $a^3 \times a^7$ .... [1]

b $a^4 \div a^{12}$ .... [1]

8 Simplify as much as possible.

a $2x^3 \times 5x^4$

.... [2]

b $\left(3x^2\right)^4$

.... [2]

c $20x^6 \div 4x^5$

.... [2]

Fractional indices

EXTENDED   NO CALCULATOR

Student's Book pages 347–351 | Syllabus learning objectives E1.7; E2.4

1 Find the value of:

a $25^{\frac{1}{2}}$ .... [1]

b $27^{\frac{1}{3}}$ .... [1]

2 Solve the equation.

$16^x = 2$ .... [1]

3 Find the value of:

a $64^{\frac{2}{3}}$

.... [2]

b $64^{\frac{3}{2}}$

.... [2]

4 Simplify:

a $x^{\frac{3}{2}} \times x^{\frac{5}{2}}$

.... [2]

b $x^{\frac{3}{2}} \div x^{\frac{5}{2}}$

.... [2]

c $\left(x^{\frac{3}{2}}\right)^4$

.... [2]

EXTENDED

Proportion

Student's Book pages 354–361 | Syllabus learning objectives E2.8

1 The time a journey takes is inversely proportional to the average speed.

When the average speed is 40 km/h the time is 25 minutes.

Find the time when the average speed is 50 km/h.

[2]

2 $p \propto t^2$. When $t = 10$, $p = 80$. Find p when $t = 30$.

[3]

3 The mass of a metal disc is proportional to the square of the diameter.

When the diameter is 4 cm the mass is 20 g. Find the mass when the diameter is 6 cm.

[3]

4 $y \propto \sqrt{x}$. When $x = 4$, $y = 30$. Find y when $x = 100$.

[3]

5 s is directly proportional to the cube of $(t + 1)$. When $t = 1$, $s = 96$. Find s when $t = 5$.

[3]

6 $a \propto \dfrac{1}{c^2}$. When $c = 0.5, y = 240$. Find a when $c = 4$.

....

.... [3]

7 d is inversely proportional to the square root of $(e - 2)$. When $e = 6, d = 12$. Find d when $e = 38$.

....

.... [3]

8 When $x = 2, y = 10$. Find the value of y when $x = 7$ if:

a y is proportional to $(x + 3)^2$

....

.... [3]

b y is inversely proportional to $(x + 3)^2$

....

.... [3]

Representing inequalities graphically

Student's Book pages 364–370 | Syllabus learning objectives E2.6

1

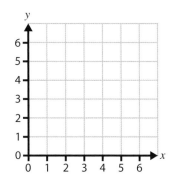

a Draw the line with the equation $y = x + 1$

.... [2]

b Shade the region where $y \leq x + 1$, $y \geq 2$ and $x \leq 4$ [2]

2

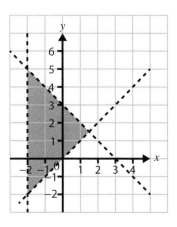

Find three inequalities to describe the shaded region on this graph.

....

....

.... [5]

3

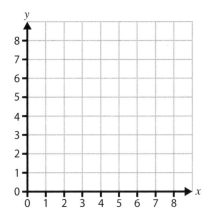

a   Draw the line $2x + y = 6$ on the grid.

.... [2]

b   Draw the line $x + 2y = 8$ on the grid.

.... [2]

c   Shade the region given by $2x + y \leq 6, x + 2y \geq 8, x \geq 0$ and $y \geq 0$ [2]

4

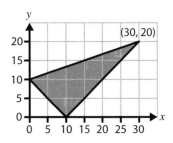

a   Find the equation of the line passing through (0,10) and (30, 20)

.... [2]

b   Find three inequalities to show the points inside the triangle.

....

....

.... [4]

Functions

EXTENDED

Student's Book pages 374–383 | Syllabus learning objectives E2.13

1 $f(x) = 2x - 5$. Work out:

a f(10) .... [1]

b f(0) .... [1]

c $f^{-1}(31)$ .... [1]

d $f^{-1}(0)$ .... [1]

2 $h(x) = 5x - 4$. The domain of h is {x: $2 \leq x \leq 7$}

Find the range of h.

.... [2]

3 $f(x) = \sqrt{x - 7}$ and $x \geq 7$

Solve the equation $f(x) = 8$

.... [2]

4 $k(x) = 2^x$. Work out:

a k(4) .... [1]

b k(−3) .... [1]

c $k^{-1}(64)$ .... [2]

5 $h(x) = 3x - 5$ and $g(x) = 10 - x$. Work out:

a $h(4)$ .... [1]

b $gh(4)$ .... [1]

c $hg(4)$ .... [1]

d Solve the equation $hg(x) = h^{-1}(x)$

....

.... [3]

6 $f(x) = 4x^2$ and the domain of f is $\{x: -1 \leq x \leq 3\}$

Work out the range of f

.... [2]

7 $f(x) = \frac{1}{2}(x + 4)$ and $g(x) = 8 - 2x$

a Find $f^{-1}(x)$

.... [3]

b Find $g^{-1}(x)$

.... [3]

c Work out $fg(1)$

.... [2]

d Write $fg(x)$ in its simplest possible form.

.... [3]

Differentiation

Student's Book pages 386–393 | Syllabus learning objectives E2.12

1

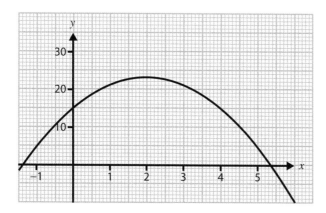

a State the coordinates of the turning point. .... [1]

b By drawing a tangent, estimate the gradient of the curve at (3, 21).

.... [3]

c By drawing a tangent, estimate the gradient of the curve at the y-intercept.

.... [3]

2 The equation of a curve is $y = x^3 - 3x^2 - 9x$

a Find the derivative $\dfrac{dy}{dx}$ .... [2]

b Find the gradient of the curve at (2, -22) .... [2]

c Find the coordinates of the turning points of the graph.

....

....

.... [5]

3 The equation of a curve is $y = x^3 - 12x$

a Find the coordinates of the turning points.

....

....

.... [5]

b State whether each turning point is a maximum or a minimum. Give a reason for your answer in each case.

....

.... [3]

4 The equation of a curve is $y = x^4 - 2x^2 + 3$

a Find the gradient of the curve at the point (2, 11)

....

.... [3]

b Show that the curve has three turning points and find their coordinates.

....

....

.... [4]

Angles

Student's Book pages 408–419 and 424–426 | Syllabus learning objectives C4.1; E4.1; C4.6; E4.6

1 *AB* is a straight line. Find the value of *x*.

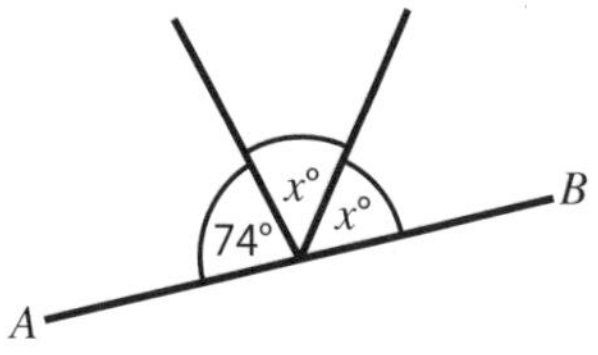

[2]

2 *AB* and *CD* are parallel lines.

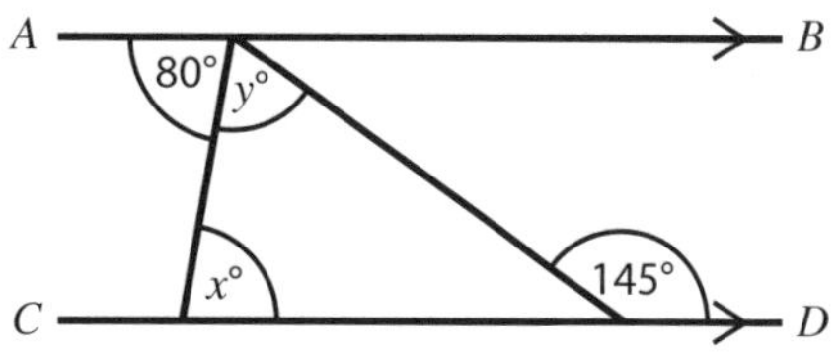

a Find the value of *x*. Give a reason for your answer.

[2]

b Find the value of *y*.

[2]

3 Three angles of a quadrilateral are each 70°. Find the fourth angle.

[2]

4 Work out the value of *t*.

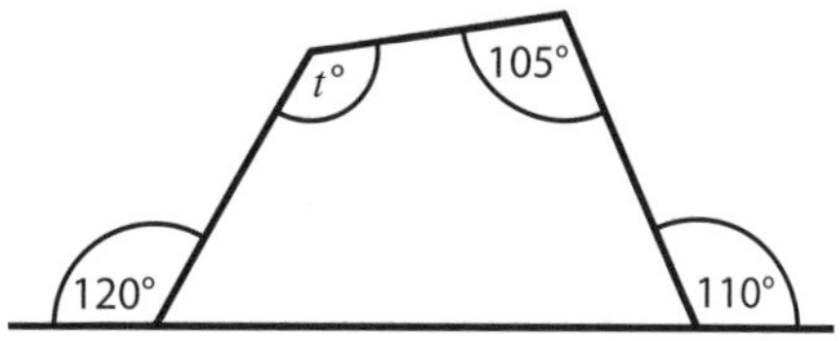

[3]

5 O is the centre of the circle.

ST is a tangent to the circle at P.

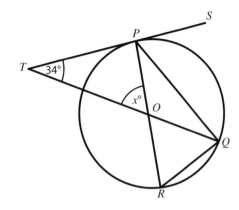

a Work out the value of x. .... [2]

b Find the size of angle PQR. .... [1]

c Explain why triangle OQR is an isosceles triangle. .... [1]

d Find the size of angle ORQ. .... [1]

Regular polygons

Student's Book pages 419–421 | Syllabus learning objectives C4.6; E4.6

1 This is a regular polygon.

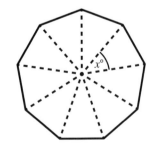

a Work out the value of x.

.... [1]

b Find the size of an interior angle.

.... [2]

2 The interior angle of a polygon is 144°. Work out the number of sides.

[2]

3 This shows four sides of a regular polygon.

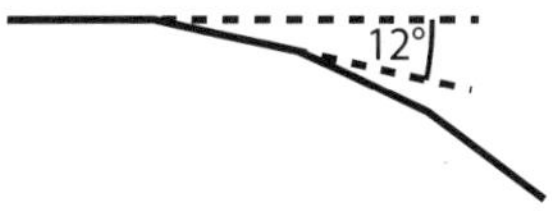

Work out the number of sides.

[2]

EXTENDED # More about polygons

Student's Book pages 422–424 | Syllabus learning objectives E4.6

1 **a** Find the sum of the interior angles of a 12-sided polygon.

[2]

b The sum of the angles of a polygon is 2700°. Work out the number of sides.

[2]

2 Four angles of a pentagon are equal.

The fifth angle is 25° smaller than each of the others.

Find the smallest angle of the pentagon.

[3]

3 This star has rotational symmetry of order 5.

Find the value of x.

....

.... **[4]**

4 The angles of a hexagon form a number sequence with a common difference of 10. Find the size of the smallest angle.

....

....

.... **[4]**

● ●

EXTENDED

Angles in circles

Student's Book pages 426–435 | Syllabus learning objectives E4.7

1 **a** Find the value of a. .... **[1]**

b Find the value of b. .... **[1]**

2 ▶ *O* is the centre of the circle.

Find the value of *x*.

Give a geometrical reason for each step in your answer.

....

.... [4]

3

a ⬤ Find the value of *x*. Give a geometrical reason for your answer.

.... [2]

b ⬤ Find the value of *y*.

.... [2]

c ⬤ Find the value of *z*.

.... [2]

4

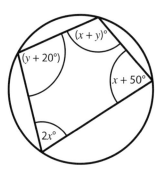

a Find the value of x.

....

....

.... [3]

b Find the largest angle of the quadrilateral.

....

.... [2]

Bearings

Student's Book pages 438–444 | Syllabus learning objectives C4.2; E4.2; C4.3; E4.3

1

A
|
|
B

AB is one side of triangle ABC.

a Measure the length of AB in centimetres. .... cm [1]

Angle A = 57° and angle B = 74°.

b Draw the triangle. [2]

2 A, B and C are three points on a map.

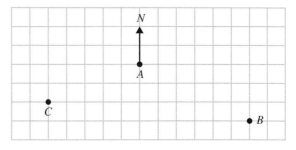

a Measure the bearing of B from A. ....° [1]

b Measure the bearing of C from A. ....° [1]

c Measure the bearing of C from B. ....° [1]

3 The bearing of P from Q is 023°.

Work out the bearing of Q from P. .... [1]

4 PQRS is a square. The bearing of Q from P is 060°.

Work out:

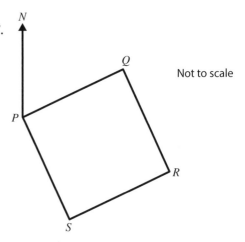

Not to scale

a the bearing of S from P .... [1]

b the bearing of R from P .... [1]

c The bearing of S from Q .... [1]

● ●

Nets

Student's Book pages 444–448 | Syllabus learning objectives C4.1; E4.1

....

1

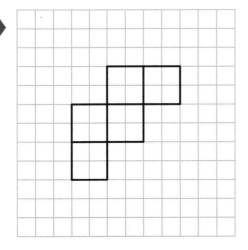

a Add a square to this diagram to make a net of a cube. [1]

b Show where a square could be added in a different place to make a different net of a cube. [1]

2 One end of a triangular prism is an equilateral triangle with a side of 4 cm.

The prism is 6 cm long.

Sketch a net of the prism.

[3]

3

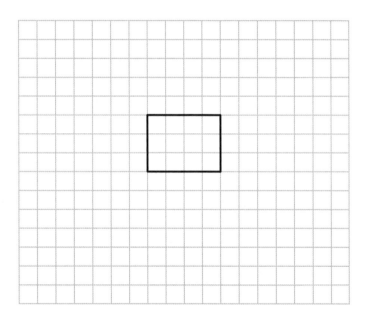

The base of a cuboid is 3 cm by 4 cm.

The volume of the cuboid is 24 cm^3.

a Draw a net of the cube. A base has been drawn for you. (On the grid above, 1 square represents 1 cm^2.) [3]

b Find the surface area of the cube.

[2]

4 This is the net of a solid.

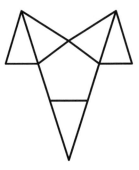

a Write down the name of the solid. .... [2]

b Find the number of vertices on the solid. .... [1]

c Find the number of edges on the solid .... [1]

Similar and congruent shapes

Student's Book pages 446-449 | Syllabus learning objectives C4.1; E4.1; C4.4; E4.4

1 Show that these two shapes are similar.

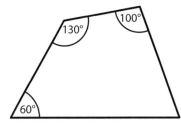 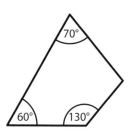

....

.... [2]

2 ▶ Shape B is an enlargement of shape A.

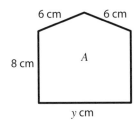
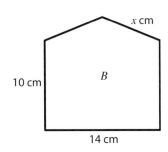

a Find the scale factor of the enlargement. .... [1]

b Find the value of x. .... [1]

c Find the value of y. .... [1]

3 ▶ Find the value of x.

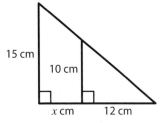

....

.... [3]

4

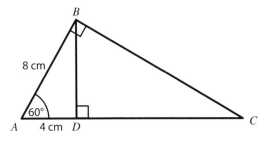

a Show that triangles ADB and ABC are similar.

....

.... [2]

b Find the length of DC.

.... [2]

Similar shapes and solids

EXTENDED

Student's Book pages 452–459 | Syllabus learning objectives E4.4

1 BC is parallel to DE. AC = 15 cm and CE = 10 cm.

The area of triangle ABC is 81 cm^2.

Calculate the area of triangle ADE.

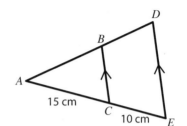

Not to scale

[2]

2 These two shapes are similar.

The area of X is 400 cm^2.

Calculate the area of Y.

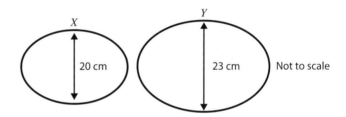

Not to scale

[2]

3 These two pyramids are similar.

The area of the base of pyramid P is 100 cm^2.

The area of the base of pyramid Q is 196 cm^2.

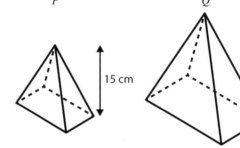

Not to scale

a The heights of the pyramids are 15 cm and x cm. Find the value of x.

[2]

b The volume of P is 500 cm^3.

Find the volume of Q.

....

.... [2]

4 All spheres are similar.

A sphere with a radius of 2.0 cm has a surface area of 50.3 cm^2 and a volume of 33.5 cm^3.

a Use this information to calculate the surface area of a sphere with a radius of 3.0 cm.

....

.... [2]

b Calculate the radius of a sphere with a volume of 100 cm^3.

....

.... [2]

Geometrical constructions

Student's Book pages 462–469 | Syllabus learning objectives C4.2; E4.2; C4.3; E4.3

1 The sides of a triangle are 5.5 cm, 6.3 cm and 7.8 cm.

Draw the triangle using a ruler and compasses only. Show your construction arcs. One of the sides has been drawn for you. [2]

5.5 cm

2 ABCD is a parallelogram.

Make an accurate drawing of the parallelogram using a ruler and compasses only.
Show your construction arcs. The diagonal AC has been drawn for you. [3]

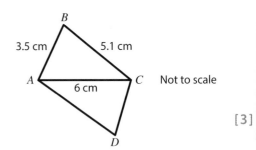

A ————————— C
     6 cm

3 XYZ is a triangular field.

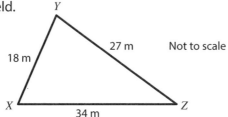

18 m

27 m   Not to scale

34 m

Make a scale drawing of the field. Use a scale of 1 cm to 5 m. [3]

4 The scale drawing shows the positions of three towns A, B and C.

A
•

Scale
1 cm represents 20 km

B •

•
C

a Find the distance from A to B in km.

.... [2]

b Find the distance from B to C in km.

.... [2]

Pythagoras' theorem

Student's Book pages 472–475 | Syllabus learning objectives C6.1; E6.1

··

1 Two sides of this triangle are 13.8 cm and 18.4 cm.

Calculate the length of the third side.

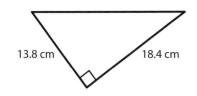

[2]

2

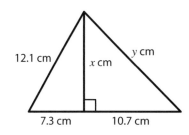

a Calculate the value of x.

[2]

b Calculate the value of y.

[2]

3 The diagram shows an isosceles right-angled triangle.

Calculate the value of x.

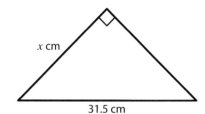

[3]

Trigonometric ratios

Student's Book pages 476–486 | Syllabus learning objectives C6.2; E6.2

··

1

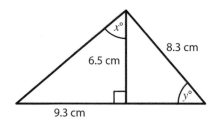

a Calculate the value of x.

.... [2]

b Calculate the value of y.

.... [2]

2 ABCD is a kite.

BD is a line of symmetry.

Calculate angle ABC.

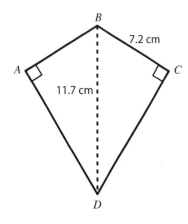

....

.... [3]

3

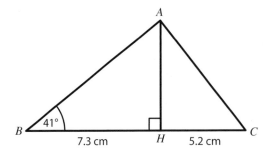

a   Calculate the height AH of triangle ABC.

.... [2]

b   Calculate the area of triangle ABC.

.... [2]

4

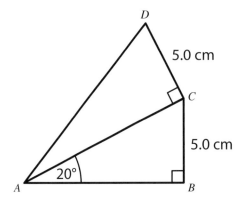

a   Calculate the length of AC.

.... [2]

b   Calculate angle DAC.

.... [2]

Exact values of trigonometric ratios

Student's Book pages 486–489 | Syllabus learning objectives E6.3

1 Find the exact value of x.

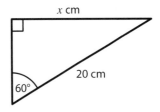

[2]

2

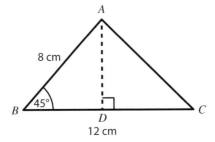

a Find the exact value of the height AD of triangle ABC.

[2]

b Show that the area of triangle ABC is $24\sqrt{2}$ cm^2

[2]

3 Simplify as much as possible $(\sin 30° + \sin 60°)^2$

[2]

4 Show that $\sin 30° + \sin 45° + \sin 60° = \frac{1}{2}(\sqrt{1} + \sqrt{2} + \sqrt{3})$

[2] **117**

Solving problems with trigonometry

Student's Book pages 489–494 | Syllabus learning objective E6.2; E6.6

1 OT is a tower. A is a point 75.0 metres from the tower on level ground.

The angle of elevation of the top of the tower from A is 53°. Calculate the height of the tower.

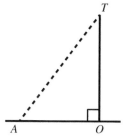

[2]

2 A ship travels from A to B, 75.2 km on a bearing of 124°.

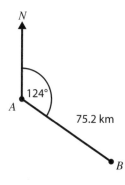

Calculate the distance that the ship travels to the east.

[3]

3 The diagram shows a cuboid. AD = 52 cm, DH = 39 cm and AB = 156 cm.

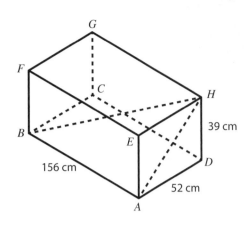

a Calculate the length of AH.

.... [2]

b Calculate the angle between BH and the base ABCD.

....

.... [3]

4 The diagram shows a pyramid with a square base ABCD with a side of 12 cm.

The vertex V is 20 cm above the centre of the base.

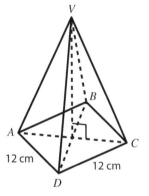

a Calculate the length of AC.

.... [2]

b Calculate the ange between VA and the base.

....

.... [3]

Sine and cosine rules

EXTENDED

Student's Book pages 495–506 | Syllabus learning objectives E6.5

1 ABC is a triangle.

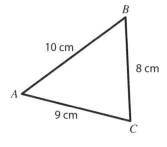

a Calculate the largest angle of the triangle.

[3]

b Calculate the area of triangle ABC.

[2]

2 X, Y and Z are three points on a map.

The bearing of Y from X is 062° and XY = 17.8 km.

The bearing of Z from X is 115° and XZ = 12.1 km.

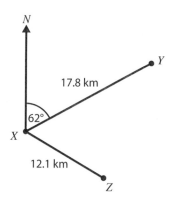

a Calculate the length of YZ.

[4]

b Work out the bearing of Z from Y.

[4]

3 Triangles ABD and CBD make the quadrilateral ABCD.

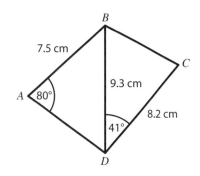

a Show that angle ADC = 93.6° to 1 decimal place.

....

....

.... [4]

b Calculate the area of the quadrilateral ABCD.

....

....

.... [4]

Trigonometric ratios of any angle

Student's Book pages 506–512 | Syllabus learning objectives E6.4

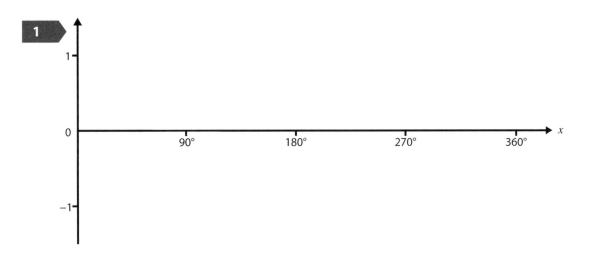

a Sketch a graph of $y = \sin x$ for $0° \le x \le 360°$ [2]

b Write down the coordinates of the turning points on the graph. [2]

c Solve the equation $\sin x = 0$ for $0° \le x \le 360°$ [2]

d Solve the equation $5 \sin x + 1 = 4$ for $0° \le x \le 360°$ [2]

2

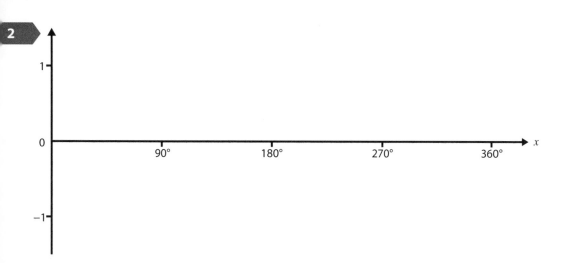

a   Sketch a graph of $y = \cos x$ for $0° \le x \le 360°$.   [2]

b   Describe the symmetry of the graph.

.... [2]

c   Solve the equation $3\cos x = 1$ for $0° \le x \le 360°$

.... [2]

d   Solve the equation $4\cos x + 5 = 2$ for $0° \le x \le 360°$

.... [2]

e   Solve the equation $(\cos x)^2 = 1$ for $0° \le x \le 360°$

.... [2]

3   **a**   Solve the equation $\sin x = \sin 35°$ for $180° \le x \le 360°$

.... [1]

b   Solve the equation $\cos x = \sin 35°$ for $0° \le x \le 360°$

.... [2]

4   Solve the equation $\sin x = \cos x$ for $0° \le x \le 360°$

.... [2]

Perimeter and area

Student's Book pages 516–525 | Syllabus learning objectives C5.2; E5.2

1 This shape is made from two congruent right-angled triangles with sides 6 cm, 8 cm and 10 cm.

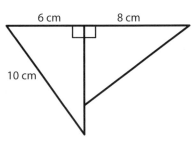

a Find the perimeter of the shape.

[2]

b Find the area of the shape.

[2]

2 A rectangular picture has sides 20 cm and 30 cm.

Round the outside of the picture is a frame 4 cm wide.

Find the area of the frame.

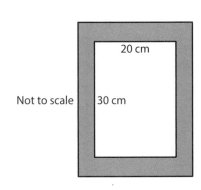

[3]

3 BC, AD and FE are parallel lines. AD is a line of symmetry.

The area of the shape ABCDEF is 210 cm^2

Work out the distance from B to F.

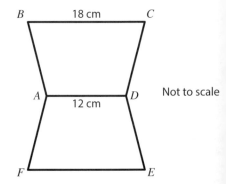

....

[3]

4

a   Work out the area of this triangle.

....   [2]

b   Work out the value of x.

....   [2]

• •

Circles

Student's Book pages 526–529 | Syllabus learning objectives C5.3; E5.3

Round calculator answers to 3 significant figures.

1   The diameter of a circle is 28 cm.

a   Calculate the circumference of the circle.

....   [1]

b   Calculate the area of the circle.

....   [2]

2 The circumference of a circular flower bed is 8 m.

a Calculate the diameter of the flower bed in metres.

.... [2]

b Calculate the area of the flower bed in m^2.

.... [2]

3 The diameter of a circular field is 30 m. X and Y are on opposite sides of the field.

A man walks in a straight line from X to Y and back again. A woman walks all round the circle from X.

The woman walks further than the man. How much further?

....

.... [3]

4 A circle of diameter 20 cm is cut out of a circle of diameter 50 cm.

Calculate the area remaining.

Not to scale

....

.... [3]

Cuboid, prism and cylinder

Student's Book pages 529–536 | Syllabus learning objectives C5.4; E5.4

1 This is the net of a cuboid on a centimetre square grid.

a Find the surface area of the cuboid.

.... [2]

b Find the volume of the cuboid.

.... [2]

2 The cross-section of this prism is a right-angled triangle.

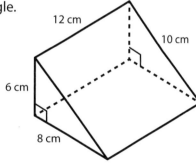

12 cm

10 cm

6 cm

8 cm

a Find the surface area of the prism.

.... [2]

b Find the volume of the prism.

.... [2]

3 The height of a cylinder is 5 cm and the cross-section is a circle with a diameter of 16 cm.

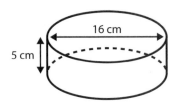

16 cm

5 cm

a Find the volume of the cylinder to 3 significant figures.

.... [2]

b Find the surface area of the prism to 3 significant figures.

....

.... [3]

4 The sides of a cuboid are 1.4 m, 2.5 m and 0.8 m.

a Calculate the volume of the cuboid.

.... [1]

b Calculate the surface area of the cuboid.

....

.... [2]

Sectors 1

Student's Book pages 536–538 | Syllabus learning objectives C5.3; E5.3

··

Round calculator answers to 3 significant figures.

1 The diagram shows a quarter of a circle.

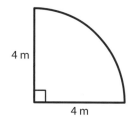

4 m

4 m

a Find the area of the shape. Leave π in your answer.

.... [2]

b Find the perimeter of the shape. Leave π in your answer.

.... [2]

2 The radius of this circle is 8.5 cm. The circle is divided into five congruent sectors.

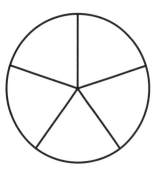

a Calculate the area of each sector.

.... [2]

b Calculate the perimeter of each sector.

.... [2]

Sectors 2

Student's Book pages 538–540 | Syllabus learning objectives E5.3

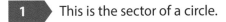

Round calculator answers to 3 significant figures.

1 This is the sector of a circle.

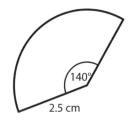

140°

2.5 cm

a Find the area of the sector.

.... [2]

b Find the length of the arc of the sector.

.... [2]

c Find the perimeter of the sector.

.... [1]

2 This is a sector of a circle. The arc length is 100 cm.

Calculate the area of the sector.

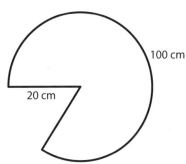

100 cm

20 cm

....

.... [3]

Pyramid, cone and sphere

Student's Book pages 540–546 | Syllabus learning objectives C5.4; E5.4

....

Round calculator answers to 3 significant figures.

1 ▶ The surface area of a sphere is 100 cm^2.

Surface area of a sphere: $A = 4\pi r^2$
Volume of a sphere: $V = \dfrac{4}{3}\pi r^3$

Calculate the volume of the sphere.

....

.... [3]

2 ▶ A pyramid has a square base and a height of 3.6 m.

The volume of the pyramid is 22.0 cm^3.

Volume of a pyramid: $V = \dfrac{1}{3}Ah$

Calculate the length of the base of the pyramid.

....

.... [2]

3 ▶ A cone has a height of 8 cm. A cut is made parallel to the base and the top part of the cone is removed. The diagram shows the remaining shape.

Volume of a cone: $V = \dfrac{1}{3}\pi r^2 h$

Curved surface area of a cone: $A = \pi r l$

4 cm
5 cm
4 cm
5 cm
6 cm

a Calculate the volume of the remaining shape.

....

.... [3]

b Calculate the surface area of the remaining shape.

....

.... [3]

4 Each side of a cube of metal is 5 cm.

The cube is melted to make spheres of diameter 8 mm.

Work out the number of spheres that can be made.

....

....

.... [5]

5 These two cones have the same volume.

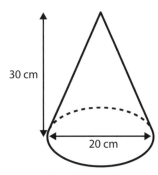
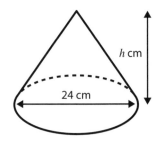

a Calculate the slant height of the first cone.

.... [2]

b Find the height h cm of the second cone.

Volume of a cone: $V = \frac{1}{3}\pi r^2 h$

....

.... [3]

Symmetry

Student's Book pages 550–554 | Syllabus learning objectives C4.5; E4.5

....

1 Draw in all the lines of symmetry in these shapes.

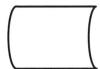 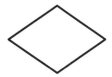

[3]

2

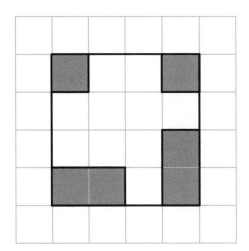

a Shade two more squares so that the shape has rotational symmetry. [1]

b Write down the order of rotational symmetry. .... [1]

3 Draw all the lines of symmetry on this shape. [2]

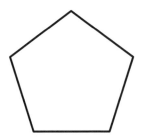

4

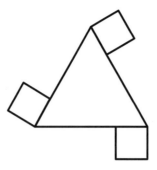

Write down the order of rotational symmetry of this shape. .... [1]

5

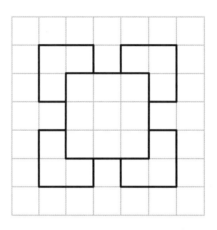

a   Draw all the lines of symmetry on this diagram. [2]

b   Write down the order of rotational symmetry. .... [1]

6   Add triangles to this diagram to make a pattern with rotational symmetry of order 6.

[2]

EXTENDED

Further symmetry

Student's Book pages 555–559 | Syllabus learning objectives E4.5; E4.8

1 This is a prism. The cross-section is an equilateral triangle.

An axis of symmetry goes through the centre of an edge and the centre of the opposite face.

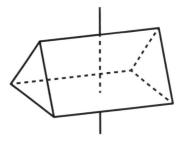

a Find the order of rotational symmetry about this axis. .... [1]

b Complete this sentence: This prism has .... axes of symmetry. [1]

c Complete this sentence: This prism has .... planes of symmetry. [1]

2 This is a cube.

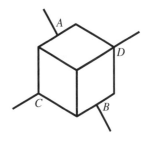

a A and B are the midpoints of opposite edges. There is an axis of symmetry through A and B.

Find the order of rotational symmetry about this axis. .... [1]

b C and D are opposite vertices. There is an axis of symmetry through C and D.

Find the order of rotational symmetry about this axis. .... [1]

3 > O is the centre of the circle. AB = CD

Find the value of x.

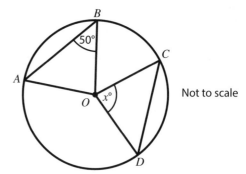

Not to scale

.... [2]

4 > AS and AT are tangents to the circle.

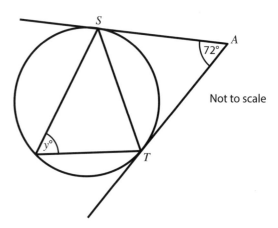

Not to scale

a What type of triangle is AST? Give a reason for your answer.

....

.... [2]

b Find angle y.

.... [2]

Transformations

Student's Book pages 562–565 and 568–571 | Syllabus learning objectives C7.1; E7.1

1

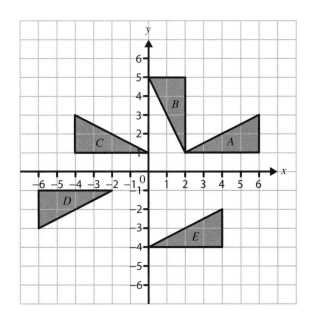

Describe **fully** the following transformations:

a *A* to *B*

.... [3]

b *A* to *C*

.... [2]

c *A* to *D*

.... [3]

d *A* to *E*

.... [2]

2

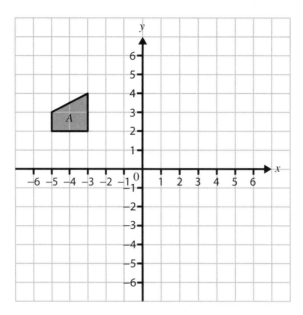

Draw the following transformations on the grid.

a   Rotate A 180° about the origin and label the result B.   [2]

b   Reflect A in the line $y = -1$ and label the result C.   [2]

c   Translate A by $\begin{pmatrix} 1 \\ -6 \end{pmatrix}$ and label the result D.   [2]

3

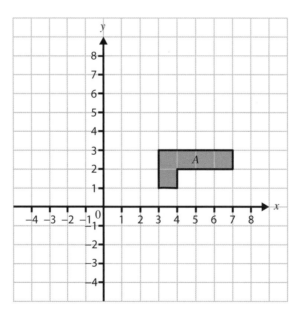

a   Rotate A 90° anticlockwise about the origin. Label the result B.   [2]

b   Rotate A 180° about (5, 3). Label the result C.   [2]

c   Rotate A 90° clockwise about (3, 1). Label the result D.   [2]

Further transformations

Student's Book pages 566–568 and 571–574 | Syllabus learning objectives E7.1

1

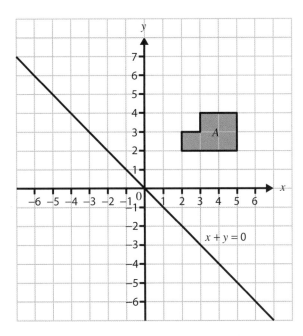

a   Draw the reflection of shape A in the line $x + y = 0$ and label the result B.   [2]

b   Draw the line $y = x + 2$ on the grid.   [2]

c   Draw the reflection of shape A in the line $y = x + 2$ and label the result C.   [2]

d   Describe fully a single transformation that maps B onto C.

[3]

2

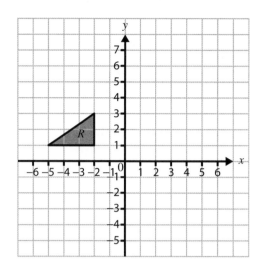

a   Rotate R 90° clockwise about (1, 1) and label the result S.   [2]

b   Rotate R 90° anticlockwise about (-1, 0) and label the result T.   [2]

c   Rotate R 180° about (-4, 3) and label the result U.   [2]

3

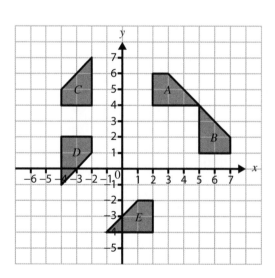

Describe fully each of these transformations:

a A onto C ....   [3]

b C onto D ....   [3]

c D onto E ....   [2]

d A onto B ....   [2]

Enlargement 1

Student's Book pages 574–580 | Syllabus learning objectives C7.1; E7.1

1

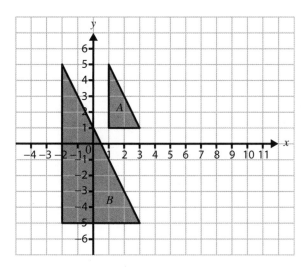

a Describe the enlargement from triangle A to triangle B.

.... [2]

b Draw the image of A after an enlargement, centre (-2, 6), with a scale factor of 2. [2]

2

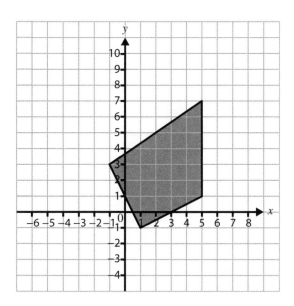

a Enlarge the shape with a scale factor of $\frac{1}{2}$ and centre (3, 3.) [2]

b Enlarge the shape with a scale factor of $1\frac{1}{2}$ and centre (1, 3). [2]

Enlargement 2

EXTENDED

Student's Book pages 580–585 | Syllabus learning objectives E7.1

1

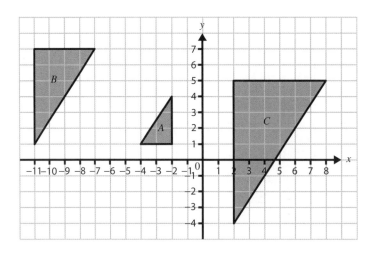

Describe the single transformation that maps

a A onto B. .... [3]

b C onto A. .... [3]

2

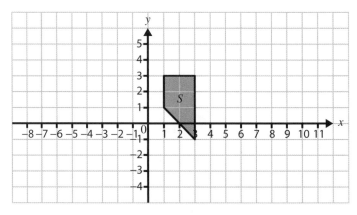

a Draw the image of shape S after an enlargement with a scale factor of $-1\frac{1}{2}$ and a centre at (-1,1). [2]

b Draw the image of shape S after an enlargement with a scale factor of $-\frac{1}{2}$ and a centre at (7, -1). [2]

EXTENDED Combined transformations

Student's Book pages 585–586 | Syllabus learning objectives E7.1

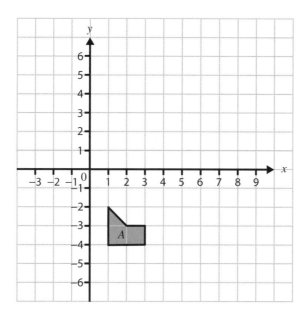

a   Enlarge A with a scale factor 2 and centre (-2, -3). Label the image B.   [2]

b   Rotate B 180° about (5.5, 0) and label the image C.   [2]

c   Describe a single transformation that maps C onto A.

[3]

2

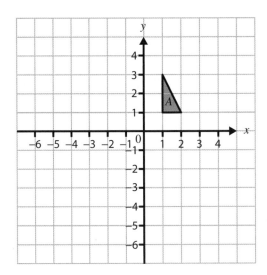

a Rotate triangle A 90° anticlockwise about (-1, -1) and label the image B. [2]

b Rotate triangle B 90° clockwise about (-6, -2) and label the image C. [2]

c Describe a single transformation that maps A to C.

.... [2]

3

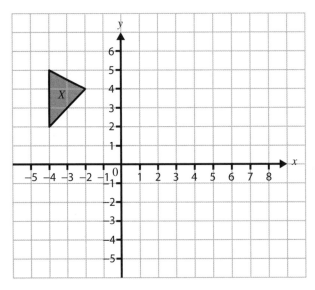

a Translate triangle X by $\begin{pmatrix} 9 \\ -5 \end{pmatrix}$ and label the image Y. [2]

b Rotate Y 180° about (2, -2) and label the image Z. [2]

c Write down a single transformation that maps X onto Z.

.... [3]

Vectors

EXTENDED

Student's Book pages 590–599 | Syllabus learning objectives E7.2; E7.3; E7.4

1 **a** Find $\begin{pmatrix} 3 \\ -2 \end{pmatrix} - \begin{pmatrix} -2 \\ 4 \end{pmatrix}$ .... [1]

b Find $4\begin{pmatrix} 5 \\ -7 \end{pmatrix}$ .... [1]

2 A has coordinates (6, 3) and B has coordinates (-2, 9).

a Write $\overrightarrow{AB}$ as a column vector. .... [1]

b Work out $|\overrightarrow{AB}|$ .... [2]

3 $XA:AY = 2:1$ and $XB:BZ = 2:1$

$\overrightarrow{XY} = \mathbf{c}$ and $\overrightarrow{XZ} = \mathbf{d}$

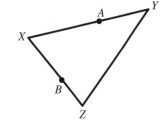

a Write $\overrightarrow{YZ}$ in terms of **c** and **d**.

.... [2]

b Write $\overrightarrow{AB}$ in terms of **c** and **d** as simply as possible.

.... [2]

c Write down two geometrical facts about AB and XY.

.... [2]

4

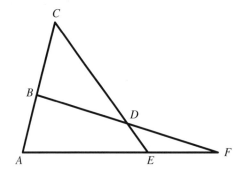

ACE is a triangle. $\overrightarrow{AC}$ = **x** and $\overrightarrow{AE}$ = **y**. B is the midpoint of AC.

$CD:DE = 3:1$ and $AE:EF = 2:1$

a Write $\overrightarrow{BD}$ in terms of **x** and **y** as simply as possible.

.... [2]

b Write $\overrightarrow{BF}$ in terms of **x** and **y** as simply as possible.

.... [2]

c Show that D is the midpoint of BF.

.... [2]

Statistical diagrams

Student's Book pages 620–633 | Syllabus learning objectives C9.1; E9.1; C9.2; E9.2; C9.4; E9.4

1 There are three parties in an election, Red, White and Blue.

This composite bar chart show the percentage of votes for each party in town A.

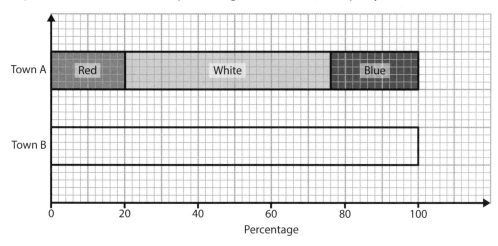

a Work out the percentage of votes for the White party in town A.

[2]

b The table shows the percentages for town B.

Party	Red	White	Blue
Percentage	44%	26%	30%

Put these results on the chart. [2]

2 ▸ This dual bar chart shows the number of boys and girls absent from school each day of one week.

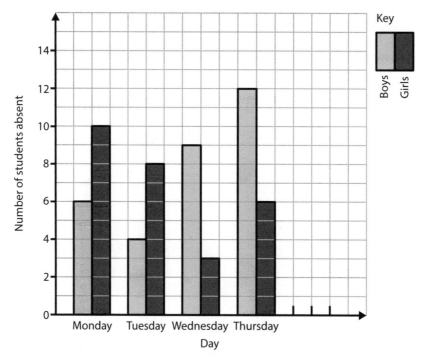

a On Friday 7 boys and 2 girls were absent. Show this on the bar chart. [2]

b Work out the total number of students absent on Tuesday.

.... [2]

c On which day was the largest number of girls absent? .... [1]

d On one day the number of boys absent was twice the number of girls absent.

What day was that? .... [1]

3 ▸ This pie chart shows the number of goals scored by 18 football teams.

Complete this table.   [3]

Goals scored	0	1	2	3	4
Number of teams					

Scatter diagrams

Student's Book pages 634–638 | Syllabus learning objectives C9.5; E9.5

1

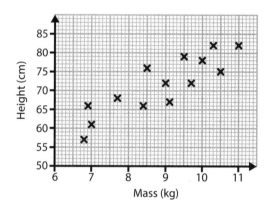

Mass (kg)

This scatter diagram shows the mass and height of some very young children.

a Here is the data for two more young children.

Mass (kg)	8.1	9.9
Height (cm)	64	76

Plot this data on the scatter diagram.   [2]

b State the type of correlation the diagram shows.

.... [1]

c Draw a straight line of best fit on the diagram.   [1]

d   Use the line of best fit to estimate the mass of a child with a height of 69 cm.

.... [1]

e   Use the line of best fit to estimate the height of a child with a mass of 9.3 kg.

.... [1]

Histograms

Student's Book pages 639–645 | Syllabus learning objectives E9.7

1   A group of people do a charity run.

This table shows their times.

Time t (min)	$20 < t \leq 30$	$30 < t \leq 35$	$35 < t \leq 40$	$40 < t \leq 50$	$50 < t \leq 70$
Frequency	15	12	21	20	16

Complete this histogram.

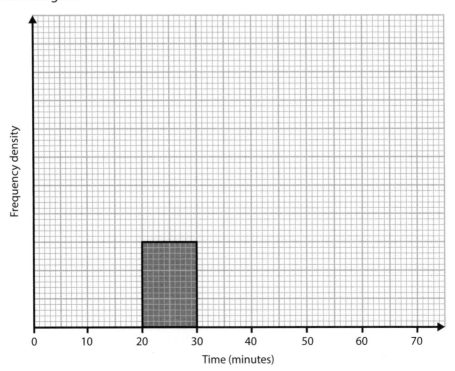

[4]

2 ▶ This histogram shows the masses of shells found on a beach.

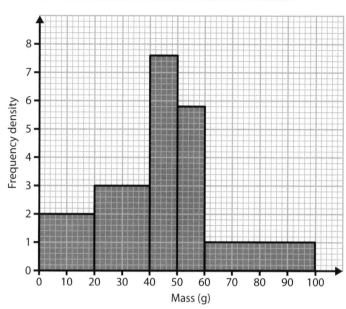

Use the histogram to complete this frequency table. [4]

Mass m (g)	$0 < m \le 20$			
Frequency				

3 ▶ This histogram shows the masses of a group of people.

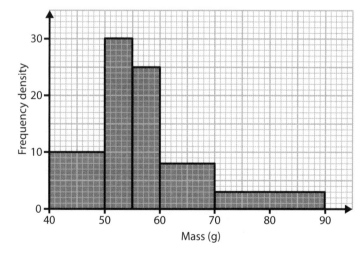

Work out how many people were in the group.

.... [4]

Averages

Student's Book pages 648–660 | Syllabus learning objectives C9.2; E9.3

1 Here are the ages of 15 children

8, 7, 11, 9, 7, 9, 7, 12, 7, 9, 8, 7, 11, 7, 6

a Find the median age.

.... **[2]**

b Find the mode of the ages.

.... **[1]**

c Find the mean age.

.... **[2]**

d Find the range of the ages.

.... **[1]**

2 20 people say how many sisters they have. The results are in this chart.

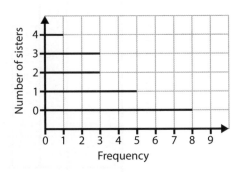

a Find the modal number of sisters. .... **[1]**

b Find the median number of sisters. .... **[2]**

3 This table shows how many days 50 people take exercise in one week.

Days	0	1	2	3	4	5	6	7
Frequency	1	2	4	12	7	6	10	8

a Find the modal number of days. .... [1]

b Show that the median is more than the mode.

.... [2]

4 **a** The mean mass of 20 people is 51.2 kg. Find the total mass.

.... [2]

b The mean mass of another 30 people is 56.7 kg. Work out the mean mass of all 50 people.

.... [2]

5 Here are seven numbers arranged from smallest to largest.

a, 10, 11, 16, b, c, 19

The range is 9 and the mode is 16.

Find the values of a, b and c.

....

.... [2]

Frequency tables and stem-and-leaf diagrams

Student's Book pages 660–667 | Syllabus learning objective C9.3; E9.3; C9.4; E9.4

1 This stem-and-leaf table shows the ages of 21 adults in a fitness class.

3	7 9 9
4	0 3 4 4 6 8
5	2 5 6 6 9
6	1 1 1 3
7	1 3 5

Key: 3 | 7 represents 37

a Find the range of the ages. .... [1]

b Find the median age. .... [2]

c Find the modal age. .... [1]

d Explain why the median is a better representative age for the class than the mode.

.... [2]

e A new person joins the class. The range is now 41. Find two possible ages for the new person.

.... [2]

2 ▶ This stem-and-leaf table shows the time, in seconds, that some students take to complete a task.

1	4 6 8 8 9	Key: 1	4 represents ....
2	0 0 1 3 6 6 8	
3		
4		

a Complete the key. [1]

b Here are five more times: 38, 44, 32, 46, 41

Put them in the stem-and-leaf table. [2]

c Find the range of the times. .... [1]

d Find the median time. .... [2]

3 ▶ This frequency table shows the number apples in 25 bags.

Number of apples	Frequency
4	10
5	8
6	3
7	2

a Write down the modal number of apples. .... [1]

b Find the median number of apples.

.... [2]

c Calculate the mean number of apples per bag.

....

.... [3]

Grouped data and cumulative frequency

Student's Book pages 668–678 | Syllabus learning objectives E9.3; E9.6

1 This frequency table shows the heights of 80 trees.

Height, h (m)	$4 < h \leq 5$	$5 < h \leq 6$	$6 < h \leq 7$	$7 < h \leq 8$	$8 < h \leq 9$	$9 < h \leq 10$
Frequency	6	11	15	22	19	7

a Write down the modal class. .... [1]

b Estimate the mean tree height.

....

....

.... [4]

c Draw a cumulative frequency graph. [3]

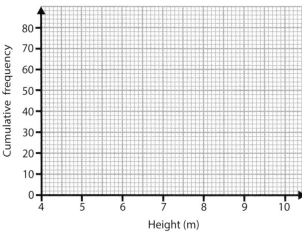

d Use your graph to estimate the median tree height. .... [1]

2 440 people complete a run for charity. Their times, in minutes, are shown on this cumulative frequency graph.

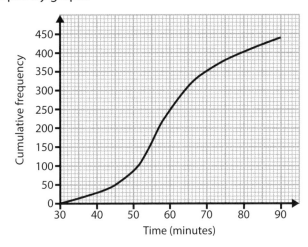

Use the graph to estimate:

a the median time

.... [1]

b the interquartile range

.... [2]

c the 15th percentile

.... [2]

d the number of runners who take more than 75 minutes.

.... [2]

Probability

Student's Book pages 682–691 | Syllabus learning objectives C8.1; E8.1; C8.2; E8.2

1 Here are nine digits: 1, 2, 3, 4, 5, 6, 7, 8, 9

One digit is chosen at random.

Find the probability that it is:

a an odd number .... [1]

b a prime number .... [1]

c not a multiple of 4. .... [1]

2 A bag contains 3 yellow beads, 6 red beads and 1 green bead.

A bead is taken from the bag at random.

Find the probability that the bead is:

a red .... [1]

b red or green .... [1]

c not green .... [1]

A bead is taken out. The colour is noted. The bead is replaced in the bag.

This is repeated 150 times.

d How many times would you expect to get a yellow bead?

.... [2]

3 A wooden cone is dropped on the floor.

It can land point up   or point down

Jan drops the cone 30 times and records the results in this table.

Outcome	Point up	Point down
Frequency	12	18

a Use Jan's results to estimate the probability that the cone lands point down. Give your answer as a percentage.

.... [2]

b If Jan drops the cone 200 times, work out how many times he expects it to land point down.

.... [2]

4 Amin catches a bus to work each morning. The probability that the bus is late is 0.15

Amin works 220 days in a year. How many times in a year does he expect the bus to be late?

.... [2]

5 A fair six-sided spinner has six different positive integers less than 10.

The probability of getting a multiple of 3 is $\frac{1}{2}$

The probability of getting a multiple of 4 is $\frac{1}{3}$

The probability of an even number is $\frac{2}{3}$

What six numbers are on the spinner?

....

.... [2]

Probability and combined events

Student's Book pages 697–705 | Syllabus learning objectives C8.3; E8.3

....

1 Carl has two boxes, A and B, of red and blue pens.

He takes one pen at random from each box.

The probability he takes a red pen from box A is 0.3

The probability he takes a red pen from box B is 0.6

a Write the missing probabilities on the branches of this tree diagram.

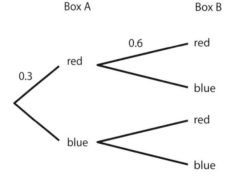

Box A   Box B

[2]

Find the probability that Carl takes:

b 2 red pens

.... [2]

c 2 blue pens

.... [2]

d 1 red pen and 1 blue pen.

.... [3]

2 In a survey, 50 students were asked if they play football or tennis.

This Venn diagram shows the results.

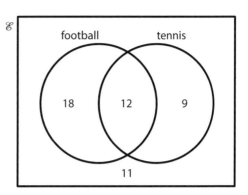

A student is chosen at random. Find the probability that the student plays:

a tennis but not football .... [1]

b neither tennis nor football .... [1]

c football and tennis .... [1]

d football... [1]

3 Rana has 20 cards numbered 1 to 20. She puts the integers from 1 to 15 in this Venn diagram.

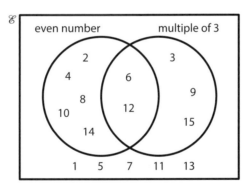

a Write the integers from 16 to 20 in the Venn diagram. [2]

Rana takes a card at random. Find the probability that it is:

b an even number or a multiple of 3 but not both .... [2]

.... [2]

c neither an even number nor a multiple of 3. .... [2]

Conditional probability

Student's Book pages 695–697 and 705–711 | Syllabus learning objectives E8.1; E8.4

1 In a survey, 200 women are asked if they can speak French or English.

The results are in this table.

		Speak French		Total
		Yes	No	
Speak English	Yes	36	104	140
	No	44	16	60
Total		80	120	200

One woman is chosen at random.

a Find the probability she can speak both languages.

.... [2]

b If the woman can speak French, find the probability that she cannot speak English.

.... [2]

c If the woman cannot speak English, find the probability that she can speak French.

.... [2]

2 Here are six cards with letters on them.

| A | A | B | B | B | C |

One card is chosen at random. It is not replaced. Then a second card is chosen at random.

a Find the probability that both cards are A.

.... [2]

b Find the probability that both cards are B.

.... [2]

c Find the probability that C is not chosen.

.... [2]

3 A test is in two parts, theory and practical. You can pass or fail each part.

The probability that a person passes theory is 0.7

If a person passes theory, the probability that they pass practical is 0.8

If a person fails theory, the probability that they fail practical is 0.9

a Write the missing probabilities on the branches of this tree diagram.

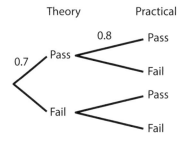

[2]

b Find the probability of passing both theory and practical.

.... [2]

c Find the probability of failing the practical.

.... [2]